The Art of Color Categorization

Kyoko Hidaka

The Art of Color Categorization

palgrave
macmillan

Kyoko Hidaka
Tokyo, Japan

ISBN 978-3-031-47689-1   ISBN 978-3-031-47690-7   (eBook)
https://doi.org/10.1007/978-3-031-47690-7

Translation from the Japanese language edition: 『色を分ける 色で分ける』 by Kyoko Hidaka, © Author 2021. Published by Kyoto University Press. All Rights Reserved.

© The Editor(s) (if applicable) and The Author(s), under exclusive license to Springer Nature Switzerland AG 2024

This work is subject to copyright. All rights are solely and exclusively licensed by the Publisher, whether the whole or part of the material is concerned, specifically the rights of reprinting, reuse of illustrations, recitation, broadcasting, reproduction on microfilms or in any other physical way, and transmission or information storage and retrieval, electronic adaptation, computer software, or by similar or dissimilar methodology now known or hereafter developed.
The use of general descriptive names, registered names, trademarks, service marks, etc. in this publication does not imply, even in the absence of a specific statement, that such names are exempt from the relevant protective laws and regulations and therefore free for general use.
The publisher, the authors, and the editors are safe to assume that the advice and information in this book are believed to be true and accurate at the date of publication. Neither the publisher nor the authors or the editors give a warranty, expressed or implied, with respect to the material contained herein or for any errors or omissions that may have been made. The publisher remains neutral with regard to jurisdictional claims in published maps and institutional affiliations.

This Palgrave Macmillan imprint is published by the registered company Springer Nature Switzerland AG
The registered company address is: Gewerbestrasse 11, 6330 Cham, Switzerland

Paper in this product is recyclable.

#BlackLivesMatter

Acknowledgements for the English Edition

In April 2020, with access to university restricted due to COVID-19, all classes were held remotely. I used this period to write this original monograph in Japanese. I know it is presumptuous of me, but I wanted to follow in the footsteps of Newton as he worked on three major achievements (prism spectroscopy, universal gravitation, and differential and integral calculus) when Trinity College, University of Cambridge was closed due to the plague epidemic in the 17th century.

At the end of May 2020, while I was teaching online classes at a closed university, an internet video showed an incident in which George Floyd was choked to death under the knee of a police officer in Minneapolis, Minnesota, US. In response, Black Lives Matter (BLM) protests and riots quickly erupted worldwide. But some Japanese media reported the cynical perversion that "blacks are poor, so they riot and steal," based solely on the scenes of violence and looting during the BLM movement. I questioned the reports that presented only fragments of the protests and looting without explaining the structural suppression of human rights and police violence against people of color over the years, starting with slavery in the first place. I sincerely wanted to convey the idea that believing this is the way it is without knowing the root causes is proof of humanity's ongoing domination by color categorization.

Ms. Shoko Nagano of Kyoto University Press challenged me with this complex global problem: "I understand the problem of color categorization, but I want a vision of what we should do from now on." I

viii ACKNOWLEDGEMENTS FOR THE ENGLISH EDITION

thank Ms. Nagano for her objective, detailed, and in-depth proofreading and Ms. Noriko Kayama for cleaning up my manuscript and organizing references with her precise suggestions. Thanks to Yohji, the incredible husband, my parents Sei and Yukiko, and my clever sister Makiko and her family, Al, Kai, and Miya, for their continuous support. Part of the research for this book was supported by JSPS Grant-in-Aid for Scientific Research (C) 18K11965: A Study of Color Standards and Nationalism for Design in Modern Britain, the Asahi Group Foundation, the J Milk, and the Mayekawa Foundation.

This book is an English translation from the original monograph in Japanese published by Kyoto University Press. The publication of this edition came about after I gave a short presentation in the Special Session "Recent Books on Colour" at the AIC 2022 Sensing Colour Conference in Toronto, Canada. My talk focused on the publication of this book in Japan, emphasizing racial and cultural diversity, a significant theme of the conference. Angélica Dass was one of the keynote speakers at the conference. After my presentation, a guest expressed her desire to read my book published in English. Inspired by her comment, I translated the text and submitted proposals to various publishers. Fortunately, Ms. Camille Davies, Senior Editor at Palgrave Macmillan, reached out to me. I would also like to thank Ms. Uma Vinesh and Ms. Chitra Gopalraj for the minute formatting of the manuscript. This is how this English edition of this book was brought to life.

National Color Day, October 22, 2023

Kyoko Hidaka

Kyoko Hidaka

CONTENTS

1 Introduction   1
  1.1 My Father and the Okinawan Fish   1
  1.2 Colorful Cakes in New York   2
  1.3 The Color of the Sun in Weather Forecasts   3
  1.4 What Is Color?   4
  1.5 On Categorization   6
  1.6 Why Did van Gogh's Color Palette Change?   7
  1.7 Color Vision of Japanese Macaques   8
  1.8 Aims of the Book   11

Part I   Categorizing Colors

2 Categorizing the Rainbow   15
  2.1 Fluctuating Number of Colors in a Rainbow   16
  2.2 Newton's Rainbow Color Discovery Through Musical Comparison   24
  2.3 Natural Fine Categorization: The Fraunhofer Line   30
  2.4 The Rainbow Flag   32

3 Categorizing Colors by Name   35
  3.1 Basic Color Terms: Their Universality and Evolution   36
  3.2 Boundaries of Color Charts   41
  3.3 Color Charts and Lighting   46
  3.4 Categorizing in Detail   49

x   CONTENTS

3.5	*Putting it Together Broadly*	54
3.6	*Increasing and Decreasing*	57
3.7	*Evolution and Eugenics*	65
3.8	*Do Basic Color Terms (BCTs) and Traditional Color Names Matter for Gender?*	68

4   Categorizing Colors by Criteria   71

4.1	*Primary Colors*	72
	4.1.1 *Red, Yellow, Blue, White, Black (R, Y, B, W, K) Theory*	73
	4.1.2 *Red, Yellow, Black, Blue (R, Y, K, B) Theory/ White, Yellow, Red, Black (W, Y, R, K) Theory*	74
	4.1.3 *Red, Yellow, Blue (R, Y, B) Theory*	75
	4.1.4 *Red, Green, Blue (R, G, B) Theory*	75
	4.1.5 *Red ↔ Green, Yellow ↔ Blue, White ↔ Black (R ↔ G, Y ↔ B, W ↔ B) Theory*	76
	4.1.6 *Red, Yellow, Green, Blue, Purple (R, Y, G, B, P) Theory*	76
	4.1.7 *Cyan, Magenta, Yellow, and Black (C, M, Y, K)*	77
4.2	*Pure Colors*	78
4.3	*Ranking*	79
4.4	*Attributes*	81
4.5	*Color Wheels and Color Spaces*	84
4.6	*Color Standards and Foods*	89

5   Categorizing Colors by Environment and Senses   93

5.1	*Temperature*	94
5.2	*Humidity*	96
5.3	*Domestic Animals*	100
5.4	*Festivals and Everyday Life*	103
5.5	*Gender*	106
5.6	*Synesthetes*	109

Part II   Categorizing Things 'by' Color

6   Categorizing Food by Color   115

6.1	*Package 1: Milk in the USA and Japan*	117
6.2	*Package 2: American and Japanese Confectionery*	120
	6.2.1 *Candy*	123
	6.2.2 *Chocolate*	123

		6.2.3	Gum	125

		6.2.3	Gum	125
6.2.4	Limited Period/Region	125
6.2.5	Blue Food Coloring and Packaging	126
6.3	Later Stories	128
6.4	Food Groups Colors	129

7 Categorizing Identities by Color — 133

7.1	Crests	134
7.2	Collar Insignia of the Japanese Military	137
7.3	Ranks	138
7.4	Sumptuary Laws	141
7.5	Landscape Laws	144

8 Categorizing People by Color — 147

8.1	Races	148
8.2	Yellow on Nazi Concentration Camp Badges	154
8.3	White, Black, and Red	159
8.3.1	Black and White	159
8.3.2	Redlining	163
8.3.3	#BlackLivesMatter	166
8.3.4	Silence Is Violence	166
8.4	Stereotypes in Film: White Saviors and Magical Negroes	168

Part III Epilogue

9 Conclusion—A Past That Ranks Colors and Refuses to Mix, and a Colorful Future — 173

References — 177

Index — 187

ABBREVIATIONS

AIC   International Colour Association
BCC   Basic Color Categories
BCC   British Colour Council
BCT   Basic Color Terms
BLM   Black Lives Matter
CMYK   Cyan, Magenta, Yellow, and Black
IAT   Implicit Association Test
ISCC   The Inter-Society Color Council
JIS   Japanese Industrial Standards
NATO   The North Atlantic Treaty Organization
NBS   The National Bureau of Standards
NCS   Natural Color System
NHK   Nippon Hoso Kyoukai (Japan Broadcasting Corporation)
RGB   Red, Green, and Blue
SS   Schutzstaffel (Protection Squadrons; a paramilitary organization within the Nazi party)

LIST OF FIGURES

Fig. 1.1	Cakes and muffins on sale in an American supermarket, Boston, MA, June 2018 (*Source* Hidaka, 2018)	3
Fig. 1.2	Van Gogh, V. Cluster of Old Houses with the New Church in the Hague [Oil painting] (1882). 34 × 25 cm. Private collection	9
Fig. 1.3	Color Palette: Twenty representative colors in Van Gogh's Painting and their plots in the 3D Adobe RGB color space (Van Gogh, V. *Road with Cypress and Star* [Oil painting] (1890). 92 × 73 cm)	10
Fig. 2.1	Primary and secondary rainbows on the horizon	17
Fig. 2.2	Terashima, Ryoan. Commentary on rainbows in Wakan Sansai Zue (1712)	18
Fig. 2.3	Hiroshige Utagawa, *Takanawa Ushimachi* (1857) woodblock print, Edo-Tokyo Museum	19
Fig. 2.4	A caricature of Louis-Bertrand Castel's ocular organ, Charles Germain de Saint Aubin (1721–1786) (*Source* Waddesdon, The Rothschild Collection [The National Trust])	27
Fig. 2.5	Chevreul, M. E. (Michel Eugène) (1864). "Plate I: Couleurs d'Un Spectre Solaire." In Des Couleurs Et De Leurs Applications Aux Arts Industriels à l'Aide Des Cercles Chromatiques. Paris, France: J.-B. Baillière et fils	31
Fig. 3.1	Color chart by Munsell Color Company attached in supplement of Basic Color Terms (1969) (*Source* Munsell Color Company)	45

xvi   LIST OF FIGURES

Fig. 3.2   Color chart by Hale Color Consultant attached
in supplement of Basic Color Terms (1999) (*Source* HALE
COLOR CONSULTANTS,INC 1989)   45

Fig. 3.3   Difference in color between incandescent and daylight
white lighting (*Source* IKEA Tokyo-Bay)   48

Fig. 3.4   Green chili peppers are packaged in English (fresh green
chili peppers) and Japanese (ao togarashi), but the blue
(ao) is not directly translated (*Source* Hidaka, K. [2017])   55

Fig. 3.5   Color categorization and gender stereotype   69

Fig. 4.1   A color wheel for urinalysis of European medical treatment
(1506) (*Source* Wellcome Collection)   85

Fig. 4.2   Appendix for students of A Color Notation (1971) (*Source*
Koji Ogata. *Note* Color panels on Munsell color system
diagram, 10 hues on the color wheel, 9 levels of lightness,
7 levels of red saturation. In the lightness steps on the left,
the white is at the top, while the black is at the bottom)   86

Fig. 4.3   Johannes Itten (1921) Color sphere in 7 light levels
and 12 tones (Die Farbenkugel) (*Source* © VG Bild-Kunst
Photo: Vitra Design Museum. *Note* 47.3 × 31.9 cm
A color illustration of Bruno Adler's Utopia depicts a color
sphere with white on top and black on the base)   87

Fig. 4.4   Color sphere of Munsell Color Company (*Source*
Massachusetts College of Art and Design. *Note* When
rotated, gray appears. Munsell's goal was to create a color
space that resembled a globe)   88

Fig. 4.5   The color tree and sphere in A Color Notation (1916)
(*Note* The concept of the Munsell color tree and color
space distorted by different saturation steps for each hue)   90

Fig. 4.6   Film color tolerance set of Hershey's Reeses produced
by Macbeth (1988) (*Source* Massachusetts College of Art
and Design. *Note* In October 1988, a chart was created
to display the tolerance of color variation with viewing
angle. The standard orange color used for Hershey's
Reeses Peanut Butter Cup packaging is defined as 9.5R
5.49/16.6. At its creation, the Macbeth Company
acquired the Munsell Color Company, which is why
the Macbeth logo appears in the lower left corner)   92

Fig. 6.1   Rainbow cookies, US East Coast   116

Fig. 6.2   Top 1–5 typical colors used for milk cartons   118

Fig. 6.3   A candy store in Tokyo (2013)   121

Fig. 6.4   The confectionery section in a supermarket in New Jersey,
US (2013)   122

LIST OF FIGURES   xvii

Fig. 6.5   Top 1–5 typical colors used in confectionery packaging   122
Fig. 6.6   Receipt from the University of Tokyo Co-op Central
Cafeteria marking three color food groups: red 2.2, green
0.3, and yellow 6.3 (2016)   130
Fig. 6.7   *"Eat the basic 7 ...: every day! eat a lunch that packs
a punch"* by the War Food Administration (1943) (*Source*
US Government Printing Office. University of Minnesota
Libraries, Upper Midwest Literary Archives)   ˙131
Fig. 7.1   Coats of arms in Italian (*Source* iStock/Duncan 1890;
Note In the top row of the eight one-color coats of arms,
from left to right, are the ovals representing the Italian,
Sicilian, French, and female coats of arms. The Portuguese,
English, and two German styles are in the lower row. The
bottom half, 12 types, are the various divided designs
of the coat of arms)   136
Fig. 7.2   Norakuro by Suiho Tagawa showcases the categorization
of military collar insignia based on color (1936)   138
Fig. 8.1   Comparison of hair color of Aryan race during Nazi
Germany (1937) (*Source* Fritz Carl [akg-images])   153
Fig. 8.2   Comparison of eye color of Aryan race during Nazi
Germany (1937) (*Source* Fritz Carl [akg-images])   153
Fig. 8.3   Skin color chart, Berlin, Germany by Prof. Dr. Felix
von Luschan (*Source* Peabody Museum of Archaeology
and Ethnology at Harvard University. *Note* 6.6 × 9.3 ×
1.4 cm. Skin color chart of 36 glass mosaic pieces set
in the double-sided brass tray with numbers; tray in brass
sleeve; marked Hautfarber-Tafel/2. Auflage nach/Prof.
Dr. Felix von Luschan/Puhl and Wagner-G. Heinersdorff/
Berlin-Treptow/Werkstatten fur Mosaik und Glasmalerei)   155
Fig. 8.4   A yellow patch to distinguish Jews (*Source* Auschwitz
Peace Museum, Fukushima, Japan)   156

xviii   LIST OF FIGURES

Fig. 8.5   Instructional material for SS guards (*Source* 25305
©Bundesarchiv, Koblenz, 146-1993-051-07. *Note*
Concentration camp insignia for protective custody
prisoners: from 1938, prisoners were categorized
by reason for detention and race, withfurther individual
subcategories. Header, from left: Political: Professional
Criminal: Emigrant: Jehovah's Witnesses: Homosexual:
Work-shy Reich: Work-shy Municipalities. Left column
from above: Basic Colors, Insignia for Recidivists:Prisoners
of the Punishment Battalion, Insignia for Jews: There
follow Special Insignia. From left: Jewish Race Defiler:
Female Race Defiler: Suspected Fugitive: Prisoner Number:
1A Prisoner. Example: Political Jew, Recidivist, Member
of thePunishment Battalion: Wehrmacht Special Operation:
P is Polish: T is Czech)   158
Fig. 8.6   British Colour Council, notes on corrections in the 1961
reprint of the Dictionary of Colour Standards (*Source*
University Library for Agricultural and Life Sciences,
the University of Tokyo. *Note* In its original publication
in 1934, BCC20 African Brown was originally spelled
using a term considered racist towards Africans. As
a response to the growing global protests against racial
discrimination and the American Civil Rights Movement
of the 1950s and 1960s, the offensive term was removed
from the name in 1961)   164

LIST OF TABLES

Table 2.1	Regional differences in the number of colors in a rainbow based on commentaries by Obayashi (1999) and Suzuki (1990)	21
Table 2.2	Categorization of a rainbow: English, Shona, and Bassa	22
Table 2.3	List of typical elements and wavelengths of Fraunhofer lines	31
Table 3.1	How Japanese indigo dyes are categorized by color names based on their lightness	51
Table 5.1	Comparison of hare and ke color schemes	104

CHAPTER 1

Introduction

And God saw that the light was good. And God <u>separated</u> the light from the darkness.

Genesis 1:4 English Standard Version (emphasis by the author)

My inquiry began with a very old question: "How do humans name or categorize a color?" But, before I touch on it, I would like to share three episodes that sparked my interest in how people in faraway places divide up colors and inspired me to write this book.

1.1 MY FATHER AND THE OKINAWAN FISH

When I was two years old, my father, who had grown up in Hokkaido, Japan, was transferred to the subtropical city of Naha in Okinawa Prefecture. He was so surprised by the colorful fish he saw for sale at the fish market in Naha that he lost his appetite and rarely ate any seafood during the entire period of his assignment. He says that he could not even imagine how he could eat bright yellow or green fish, having grown up in an environment where blue fish were the norm and red fish were for celebrations. The dye scholar Ujo Maeda (1880–1960)[1] wrote that human beings' instincts, especially those of appetite, and the perception

---

[1] Maeda, U. (1980). *Color: Dye and Color*. Hosei University Press, p. 6.

© The Author(s), under exclusive license to Springer Nature
Switzerland AG 2024
K. Hidaka, *The Art of Color Categorization*,
https://doi.org/10.1007/978-3-031-47690-7_1

of color are interrelated. This story of my father was an embodiment of this.

1.2   Colorful Cakes in New York

My own interest in color began when I was 16 years old. My father was posted to New York, and my mother, my younger sister, and I moved with him to the United States. The first thing that struck me was the cakes sold in supermarkets (Fig. 1.1). These cakes were decorated with artificially bright green, blue, and pink icing; the range of color they displayed was quite different from that of Japanese cakes, and they tasted much sweeter and blander. Before I moved to New York, I had the naïve delusion that American cakes must be more sophisticated in taste and appearance than Japanese ones. I was surprised to find my fantasies betrayed. Still, I gradually became accustomed to the American sense of color and taste, they became part of my everyday life, and within a year I was eating cake without even thinking about it. Today, although cakes with brightly colored ingredients are sold in Japan, they cannot compare with the vividness of American coloring.

Einstein said, "Common sense is the collection of prejudices acquired by age eighteen." At age 16, according to Einstein's measure, I must have acquired a nearly complete collection of prejudices, approaching 90%. This is no doubt why I was surprised by the colors of American cakes: they were so far removed from the stereotypes or common sense that I had had until then. Looking back, my father and I were probably subject to the stereotypes of color categorization that had been instilled in us, according to which the color of edible fish, or cake, should (or should not) be a certain way, imposing the idea that other regions should also have the same conception. My father in Hokkaido and I in Tokyo grew up thinking that bright orange and green fish or bright synthetic blue and pink sponge cakes were not edible. While there are individual differences across individuals' likes and dislikes, stereotypes of human color categories are nurtured, changed, and adapted by the environment in which we live. I eventually got used to and adapted to the colors of American cakes (although I still do not think they taste that good).

Fig. 1.1 Cakes and muffins on sale in an American supermarket, Boston, MA, June 2018 (*Source* Hidaka, 2018)

1.3 The Color of the Sun in Weather Forecasts

Color expressions common in Japan may have different counterparts in other countries. Living in the US, I experienced firsthand that many things, such as climate, food, culture, and education, influence how we see and express color. The color of the Sun, as depicted in TV weather forecasts, differs between cultures. In Japan, weather forecasts depict the Sun as red, but it is shown in yellow or orange elsewhere. All these are representations, as the Sun appears white or yellow during the day and red at sunset. However, this does not explain who chose the color of the Sun for a country's weather forecast.

These considerations led me to investigate the communication of color and to become involved in research. My laboratory is called the Color and Communication Design Laboratory. Simply put, color communication is the subject that asks, "How do we convey the information of the colors we see to others?" If your classification of color does not match the classification of the person you are trying to communicate with, the information will not be conveyed accurately. There are many ways to convey color information, such as using objects as metaphors, pointing to a chart, or assigning names, symbols, or numerical values to colors. This is the subject of my life-long research.

I have often pondered the theories surrounding the communication of color. Some people believe that universal color terms and categories apply to all cultures. However, this viewpoint, which was once more popular in Japan, has been presented in a prescriptive manner and needs to be examined in the light of other theories. Moreover, the number of basic color terms and categories has been revised over time.

This book discusses a range of color terms and categorizations. The central axis of the discussion revolves around an expansion of the considerations in *Basic Color Terms: Their Universality and Evolution* by Berlin and Kay (1969). *Basic Color Terms*, which marked a milestone in the study of color and language, is a groundbreaking study demonstrating that humans share a focal color concept and basic color categories that transcend language; there is a common evolutionary pattern in color names. Their analysis, which draws on extensive interpersonal research and linguistic reconstruction, has influenced cultural anthropology, linguistics, and cognitive psychology. In this book, I examine the debates that have emerged from research into the use of color terms and identify novel issues for debate and research.

1.4   What Is Color?

In one of her studies on basic color terms, Anna Wierzbicka notes that many languages in Australia, Papua New Guinea, and Africa do not have a word for color. She argues that while color constitutes a distinct and essential concept for English, Japanese, and many other languages, it is not a universal concept.[2] In a society with no concept of color, there

---

[2] Wierzbicka, A. (2006). The Semantics of Colour: A New Paradigm, p. 2.

1 INTRODUCTION 5

would necessarily be no concept of color names or categorization of colors. The naturalness of the concept of color and the tendency to classify colors may itself be a stereotype learned from the environment in which one was raised.

What does it mean to see color? Three essential elements enable human perception of color. If any one of these is missing, it is impossible.

1. Eye: vision/sight
2. Light: light source, brightness (exceptions: light seen in dreams, flickering light when eyelids are pressed, colors seen due to medication side effects, etc.)
3. Color: object, light source color, surface color, transmitted color, etc. (other color phenomena such as scattering, refraction, diffraction, interference, etc.)

Because the object and the illuminating light have color, color is perceived through the synergistic effects of both the object and the light. Let us compare this with the definition of color found in Japanese Industrial Standards (JIS).

1. An attribute of visual perception consisting of a combination of chromatic and achromatic components. The names of chromatic colors include yellow, orange, red, pink, green, blue, and purple, and those of achromatic colors include white, gray, and black; most color names can be modified by the additional terms light or dark and can be combined with other color names.
2. Color stimuli can be defined using three numerical values with specified calculation methods: psychophysical color, color stimulus, and color tristimulus values.[3]

The first definition above divides color into two broad categories, chromatic and achromatic colors, and indicates that names and adjectives express them. The second definition may appear confusing, describing the reduction of color stimulus to sets of three numbers. For both, however, to communicate a color to others, we use a name, adjective, quantity,

[3] JIS Z 8105:2000 "Terminology Related to Color," No. 2001 "Color."

6   K. HIDAKA

or symbol. When a name, adjective, quantity, or symbol is attached to a color, it is recognized as different from other colors and can be classified.

1.5   ON CATEGORIZATION

People consider red a warm color and blue a cool one. It is also common to use color to categorize items that are difficult to distinguish otherwise. For example, people use colored sticky notes and labels to distinguish differences in content by color. The logic of color categorization is a keynote theme of this book.

Categorization refers to distinguishing between things as being related or distinct. The act of categorization itself is part of culture, that is, categorization criteria reflect culture, as noted by the anthropologist Katsuyoshi Fukui (1943–2008).[4] Categorization may include a hierarchical structure of large and small divisions, categories, and genres, which vary by culture, period, and field. The logic of such a system also generates variations at the national, period, and individual levels. These variations are likely the source of the diversity of categorization criteria.

For example, a general judgment is relatively universal: the night sky is dark, and blood is red. However, diversity is seen with each region's climate, vegetation, and lifestyle concerns. For instance, in Japan, apples are generally red, but in England and France, apples are green, and the color name "apple green" is common. Similarly, the use of differentiated words to describe color of things in different countries creates diversity in categories and expressions.

According to Sahlins, the evolution of societies is generally of two types, general and specific. Adaptation to a specific natural environment shapes the technology and lifestyle of the culture in that environment. General evolution refers to the tendency for language and society to become more organized and complex as humans adapt to their environment. Specific evolution, by contrast, refers to the adaptation to the environment that results from interaction with other cultures and the uniqueness of the local environment. The result of these various

---

[4] Fukui, K. (1991). *Recognition and Culture: An Ethnography of Color and Pattern*, pp. 30–32.

1 INTRODUCTION   7

adaptations, according to Sahlins' account, which I consider correct, is diversity.[5]

Much information that influences our lives comes through our eyes, and color is particularly important. In an everyday example, a traffic lane can be crossed based on the color information in a sign that changes from red to green. Can one's perception and expression of colors remain constant or evolve throughout one's lifetime? How common is this to all humans, and what leads to human diversity? There are many theories on this point. For many, blindness, vision loss, and accompanying changes in color vision can occur due to disease, aging, surgery, trauma, and other causes. Other changes may also take place. In an environment different from the one in which we were born and raised, our perception and categorization of color may change as we adapt to the color sense of the people around us and the new climate, environment, education, diet, and other factors.

For example, how does ambient light (natural or artificial) affect how humans perceive color? The following two examples indicate the possibility that one's environment and education can change color perception and, conversely, that color perception acquired in childhood can become fixed.

1.6   WHY DID VAN GOGH'S COLOR PALETTE CHANGE?

The painter Vincent Willem van Gogh (1853–1890) was born in Zundert, the Netherlands but moved to Paris to pursue art. Van Gogh's painting style and coloring changed radically over the short period of his move from Nuenen to Paris.

Figure 1.2 shows the color scheme of van Gogh's Dutch period landscape painting *Cluster of Old Houses with the New Church in The Hague* (1882). The overcast sky, shadowy ground, and contrasts in this painting are not the same as those in Van Gogh's French period. It is hard to believe that this was painted by the same artist. Van Gogh lived with his brother, an art dealer, in Paris, and then he moved to Arles in southern France, following which he was committed to a mental hospital in Saint-Rémy-de-Provence. In one of his last landscapes from the Saint-Rémy period, *Road with Cypress and Star* (1890) (Fig. 1.3), there is a slight

[5] Sahlins, M. (1960). "Chapter 3: Adaptation and Stability." In *Evolution and Culture*, pp. 45–68.

resemblance to the Dutch period in the ochre and brown, but the expansion of the color range to gray and blue, and the brushwork show a stark difference.

It is easy to imagine that France's sunlight, food, scenery, and available paints differed from those in the Netherlands. In addition, van Gogh's encounters with French Impressionist painters must have prompted a change in his painting style. We cannot help but feel that the environment to which van Gogh emigrated dramatically impacted his vision and was behind this drastic change in color.

In the movie *China's van Goghs*,[6] Xiaoyong (a Chinese man living near Dafen Village in the city of Shenzhen, China), who for over 20 years has been painting replicas of van Gogh's paintings for sale as souvenirs in the Netherlands, actually sees the bright blue night sky and yellow café terrace in Arles for the first time in his life and is impressed by these colors, which, in his words, are "the same as the painting." These differed from the colors of the everyday scenery of Shenzhen, where Xiaoyong lived. For van Gogh, the strong yellow and blue colors of Arles may have been rare in the Dutch night. It is possible that van Gogh's change in approach to color was accelerated by the change in the night sky he saw.

Whether van Gogh's genius and madness in painting can be applied to other human beings is beyond the scope of this book. However, we can infer from the changing nature of van Gogh's paintings the possibility that the environment in which we live can change our color expression, even after we reach adulthood. Humans may adapt to the colors they see in their living environment as they live their lives.

1.7 COLOR VISION OF JAPANESE MACAQUES

Some primates have trichromatic color vision and can communicate with humans. The following experimental report shows how, once acquired, color vision can become fixed. Japanese macaques reared for one year in a monochromatic light environment, where they could only judge brightness, could not distinguish between cards of similar colors to the lights. Furthermore, they did not recover from this color discrimination disorder

---

[6] Yu Haibo, Yu Tianqi Kiki, *China's van Goghs* (2016).

1 INTRODUCTION

Fig. 1.2 Van Gogh, V. Cluster of Old Houses with the New Church in the Hague [Oil painting] (1882). 34 × 25 cm. Private collection

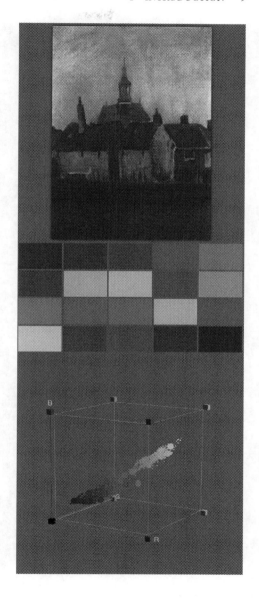

Fig. 1.3 Color Palette: Twenty representative colors in Van Gogh's Painting and their plots in the 3D Adobe RGB color space (Van Gogh, V. *Road with Cypress and Star* [Oil painting] (1890). 92 × 73 cm)

even after later training.[7] Although it remains a question whether the development of color vision is the same in macaques and humans, this experiment indicates the possibility that once color vision is determined, it may not be possible to change it later in life.

I take the view that most humans are born with universal color vision (trichromatic in the normal range). As they mature in different environments in different parts of the world, their color vision and expression diversify, influenced by climate, culture, and other factors.

1.8　Aims of the Book

In this book, I explore how color categorization criteria are both universal and diverse, influenced by factors such as environment, climate, culture, and education. The book is divided into two parts. Part I describes the division of color itself, and Part II describes the division of some objects by (using) color.

Part I introduces the categorization of colors using a rainbow, color names, ranks, and attributes. There are many color charts that represent the color system, the order in which colors are classified, and the tools used to classify them. A color order system is a system[8] in which colors are given positions and sorted in topological space (i.e., a set plus certain information) to order colors and in which the system is logically organized and described using numerical values and symbols. A color chart is a table of colors or an array of color samples. Many beautiful, well-designed examples of color charts have been produced. These originated from samplers for dyeing, weaving, printing, etc.

In Part II, I consider the universality and diversity of color categorizations, using a comparison of color schemes for milk and confectionery packages in the US and Japan as an example. I explain how the division of class and rank is reflected in color labels. Finally, I examine the ultimate friction caused by the division of people by skin color: racism.

There is one hypothesis that I elucidate while reviewing the various theories of color categorization standards. Namely, *what similarities and differences are there between Western color categorization and the logic of*

---

[7] Sugita, Y. (2004). Experience in Early Infancy is Indispensable for Color Perception. pp. 1267–1271.

[8] Caivano, J. L., & Nemcsics, A. (2022). Color Order Systems, p. 1.

racism? I show that establishing and using the color chart as a tool for color categorization delineates the path of color science and color theory; at the same time, behind its development, a way of thinking that is also humane emerges.

This book focuses on the themes of color theory, a course I taught at a university. This course, in which communicating and understanding color were examined with design students, is generally offered in both Japanese and English. Because the English class is small and mainly made up of international students, it is possible to have discussions based on the situation in other countries. Once, I was asked by a student what I was researching, and I replied, "Color theory, I am most interested in color charts, especially in the logic analysis of color charts and categories." The student continued, "Is that science? Or arts and humanities?" I am still confronted with this question. Having taught in art and design, I am still unsure which camp my academic approach to color falls into. In this book, I take a perspective on color culture.[9] The academic field of color culture is a fusion of art, anthropology, history, linguistics, and psychology. The literature and articles on color categorization criteria reviewed in this book are, necessarily, cross-disciplinary and interdisciplinary.

Before discussing universality and diversity in color categorization, it is necessary to see that categorization has two sides: a dividing to focus on differences and a connecting to focus on commonalities.[10] I see the universality here and how it connects people while, at the same time, I keep an eye on diversity and think about how categorization should be carried out. I hope this book will guide all toward a better appreciation of both the similarities and differences between our own perspectives and those of others elsewhere around the globe.

---

[9] The term "color culture" was first used in Japan by Maeda Yukichika (1880–1960). Maeda wrote *A History of Japanese Color Culture* (1960) and *Murasaki-kusa: A Cultural-Historical Study of Japanese Colors* (1956), dealing with Japanese color names and dyeing. Art historian John Gage (1938–2012), who wrote *Colour and Culture: Practice and Meaning from Antiquity to Abstraction* (1993) from the interdisciplinary perspective of the development of color studies and its relationship to art, popularized the name "color culture" as an academic field worldwide.

[10] Minaka, N. (2017). *Systematics of Thinking: Diagrammology from the View of Classification and Systematics*, p. 98.

PART I

Categorizing Colors

CHAPTER 2

Categorizing the Rainbow

I have set my rainbow in the clouds, and it will be the sign of the covenant between me and the earth. Whenever I bring clouds over the earth and the rainbow appears in the clouds.

Genesis 9: 13–14, New International Version

How do we divide a rainbow and allocate names to its colors? Many people are thrilled when they see a rainbow in the sky after rainfall, with all the colors at once. Rainbows are a universal phenomenon, but it has been said that the number of color divisions depends on culture and language. This chapter first considers the colors humans use to divide the rainbow, which, in the Biblical book of Genesis, is a sign of God's covenant not to cause a future flood on a scale that would destroy humanity.[1] However, the Bible does not specify the number of colors in a rainbow.

A rainbow is an optical phenomenon due to sunlight that can be seen in many parts of the Earth. It appears as an arc-shaped band of color reflected from water droplets and clouds in the air illuminated by the Sun. The sequence of colors in a rainbow is called a spectrum, derived from the Latin *specere* (to see) and *spectrum* (image).[2] I will explore how this spectrum is categorized.

---

[1] Genesis 9: 12–17.

[2] Takemoto, K., & Kanaoka, K. (1986). *The Etymology of Chemistry*, p. 212.

© The Author(s), under exclusive license to Springer Nature Switzerland AG 2024
K. Hidaka, *The Art of Color Categorization*,
https://doi.org/10.1007/978-3-031-47690-7_2

2.1 Fluctuating Number of Colors in a Rainbow

Cultural anthropology and ethnology have extensively focused on the number of colors in a rainbow as a subject of study. Ethnographer Taryo Obayashi (1929–2001) conducted a detailed study of the traditions associated with the rainbow worldwide and what colors people consider constitute it. Obayashi observed that some cultures regard the rainbow as a snake, a dragon, a bow, a path, a bridge, or a belt. In the Amami region in Japan, rainbows traditionally consist of two colors, red and blue, but in East Asia, five colors seem to be a common belief.[3] The Chinese character for rainbow means "snake" and is an ideograph depicting a rainbow as a snake that pierces the sky. In East Asia, a rainbow also means a five-colored flag.

The Kamakura-era history book *Azuma Kagami* describes a rainbow as having five colors:

> *In the west, I see a five-colored rainbow. The upper layer is yellow, the next five feet or more* [approximately 151.5 cm] *is red, the next is blue, the next is red plum blossoms, and the middle layer is red. The rainbow's colors are reflected in the sky and earth, and in a short time, the rain will fall.*
>
> June 11, 1218, Volume 23

The sequence of rainbow colors described in *Azuma Kagami* is "yellow, red, blue, red plum blossoms (presumably purple or violet) and red," which is different from the well-known textbook order (red–orange–yellow–green–blue–indigo–violet). Yellow is the outermost color of this rainbow in *Azuma Kagami*. There is also no mention of green, perhaps equated with blue; orange does not appear in a rainbow either. Color names also differ from today's, with purple being called red plum blossoms in the Kamakura period (1185–1333). Red repeatedly appears, causing a double rainbow (the outer rainbow is called a secondary rainbow, and the color order is reversed; Fig. 2.1). However, in an era with no prisms or color photography, people would have found it extremely difficult to carefully observe and count the number of colors of a rainbow, which appeared in the sky only for short periods. It may have been some other meteorological phenomenon.

---

[3] Obayashi, T. (1999). *Ginga no Michi: Niji no Kakehashi. (The Way of the Galaxy, Bridging the Rainbow)*, p. 232.

Fig. 2.1 Primary and secondary rainbows on the horizon

According to "Japanese Meteorological Records" in *Weather History of Japan*,[4] only 100 rainbow observations were recorded between 644 and 1876, including 41 white rainbows, and two of them were five-color[5] and six-color[6] rainbows.

The encyclopedia of the Edo period (1603–1868), *Wakan Sansai Zue*, edited by Ryoan Terashima, describes a rainbow (Fig. 2.2) by comparing it to a snake or dragon. The male was called a rainbow (虹),

---

[4] Central Weather Bureau and Marine Observatory (Eds). (1976). *Weather History of Japan 2, Vol. 11: "Rainbows and Halo"*, pp. 655–665.

[5] "Five-Color Rainbow," June 1218.

[6] "Six-Color Rainbow," June 837.

18   K. HIDAKA

while the female was called another rainbow (メ), and the primary and secondary rainbows were regarded as a male–female pair. The black-and-white illustration shows primary and secondary rainbows with three or five colors connected by dotted lines. Japanese people in the Edo period also believed that the red color of the rainbow was made of fire, while the green was made of water.

None of the observations and depictions of rainbows during the Edo period mentioned the seven colors. The rainbow in Hiroshige Utagawa's

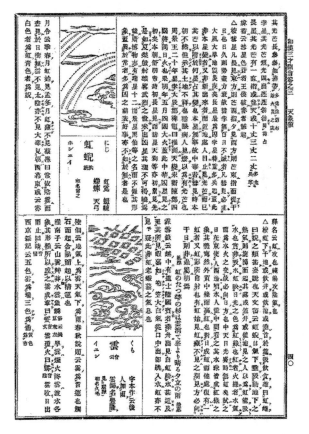

Fig. 2.2 Terashima, Ryoan. Commentary on rainbows in Wakan Sansai Zue (1712)

ukiyoe print *Takanawa Ushimachi* (1857) is not demarcated but has only three to four colors: red, yellow, and blue. In the foreground are two discarded watermelon rinds paired with a rainbow. These rinds were green and yellowish-white, with red fruit (Fig. 2.3).

Although the concept of a seven-color rainbow may have been widespread among the educated classes through Dutch scholars that appeared in the Edo period, it is reasonable to assume that the majority of the Japanese population believed that rainbows usually have five colors. Linguistic sociologist Takao Suzuki (1926–2021) argued that in Japan, rainbows had long been determined to consist of seven colors.[7] Still, in response to Suzuki's seven-color theory, Obayashi quoted *Azuma Kagami*, and questioned whether the Japanese rainbow traditionally had

Fig. 2.3 Hiroshige Utagawa, *Takanawa Ushimachi* (1857) woodblock print, Edo-Tokyo Museum

---

[7] Suzuki, T. (1990). *Japanese and Foreign Languages*, p. 98.

five colors.[8] On the basis of the encyclopedia *Wakan Sansai Zue* and the print *Takanawa Ushimachi*, one can infer that rainbows did not yet have seven colors during the Edo period.

Let us now discuss the number of rainbow colors in Europe, which has varied from popular mythology to scientific literature. Obayashi wrote that since ancient times, a wide range of cultures has existed in Europe, including Scandinavian, German, and French, that regard the rainbow as having three colors.[9] For instance, according to Kunihiko Sugiyama, who collected and introduced literature on rainbows from ancient and modern times, the colors of the rainbow in the Norse mythological Edda (songbooks and poetry) were red (fire), green (water), and blue (air), and the component attributes of each color were also indicated.[10] From these three colors of ancient legend, the number of colors gradually increased throughout Europe, reaching almost an upper limit of seven, according to the English scientist Isaac Newton (1642–1727).[11] Nevertheless, in *Opticks: or, A Treatise of the Reflexions, Refractions, Inflexions and Colours of Light* (1704), Newton recognized that there are in sunlight "innumerable other intermediate sorts of rays," making clear that the seven named colors were in fact arbitrary divisions of a continuum.

Suzuki explained the number of colors in a rainbow in European languages. In British English, scientific literature is unified with seven colors, following Newton's theory, whereas popular literature uses six colors, and the number fluctuates. French textbooks and dictionaries commonly use seven colors, while many German works use five. Russian uses a range of four to seven depending on the type of literature (folklore stories or scientific literature).[12]

Table 2.1 summarizes the number of colors in a rainbow in various parts of the world, taken from the discussions by Suzuki and Obayashi. The range of such colors is not included in the table but is limited to the number of classification categories (i.e., how many rainbow colors are categorized into how many numbers). This is because the rainbow color range (i.e., what colors of the rainbow are categorized and where) may

---

[8] Obayashi, T. (1999). *The Way of the Galaxy, Bridging the Rainbow*, p. 710.

[9] Obayashi, T. (1999). *The Way of the Galaxy, Bridging the Rainbow*, p. 560.

[10] Sugiyama, K. (2013). *A Picture History of the Rainbow*, p. 307.

[11] Sugiyama, K. (2013). *A Picture History of the Rainbow*, p. 19.

[12] Suzuki, T. (1990). *Japanese and Foreign Languages*, pp. 80–91.

2 CATEGORIZING THE RAINBOW   21

vary from one ethnic group to another and from one region to another in detail. For example, even if continental Southeast Asia and West Asia follow a four-color categorization, this does not necessarily mean they draw these colors at the same point in the rainbow.

Let us look at some examples of studies that explore the division of rainbow colors in Africa. Table 2.2 shows a diagram of Gleason's partitioning of the rainbow.[13] Gleason's *An Introduction to Descriptive Linguistics* (1955) showed the rainbow demarcation ranges for English, Shona (a language used in Zimbabwe, Mozambique, and Zambia in southern Africa), and Bassa (a language used in Liberia and Sierra Leone in Western Africa).[14] Gleason's native language, American English, classifies the rainbow as having six colors, Shona three colors, and Bassa two colors.[15] Rainbows in Shona consist of three colors, $cips^w$ uka—which

Table 2.1 Regional differences in the number of colors in a rainbow based on commentaries by Obayashi (1999) and Suzuki (1990)

Region	Number of colors
East Asia	2–7 (red and blue 2 in Amami, 5 in Chinese tradition, 7 for the Miao people of Southeast Sichuan)
Southeast Asian Continent	4 (for the Sherdukpen people of Assam in northeastern India)
Southeast Asian Islands	2–4 (4 for Taiwan, the Philippines, and Eastern Indonesia)
Oceania	No color number classification, identical to blood
North and Central Asia	5 for Siberia and Tibet; distinction between summer and winter rainbows for the Ainu
North America	1 (winter rainbow) and 3 (summer rainbow); 6 for the United States
Central and South America	Varies from person to person; basic is red and blue, 2–4 colors
Europe	3–7 (5 for Germany, 4–5 for Russia, 6 for England, 7 after Newton's theory became popular)
Africa	2–8 (multicolored for the Maasai, 7 for the Dogon, 8 for the Aru tribe)

[13] In mid-twentieth-century linguistics, Gleason's *Descriptive Linguistics* was a must-read introduction to linguistic analysis. The classification of the colors of the rainbow was used as an example of linguistic relativism.

[14] Gleason (1955). "Shona and Bassa," p. 7.

[15] Suzuki, T. (1990). *Japanese and Foreign Languages*, pp. 65–66.

22   K. HIDAKA

refers to both the red-to-orange spectrum and the purple spectrum—*citema*, and *cicena*.

Meanwhile, the Bassa rainbow has only two colors, *hui* and *ziza*, because the Bassa categorization follows only two colors, yellow (xanthic) and blue (cyanic). Gleason stated that this two-color taxonomy is also common in the Western European classification of plant colors. The yellow/blue dichotomy is also typically used as a temperature sensor, distinguishing warm and cold colors. Thus, different languages at different periods put dividing lines on the rainbow in different places.

Modern Japanese people almost always state that the rainbow has seven colors as a result of education derived from England in the early Meiji period. From the end of the Edo period to the Meiji period, a trial-and-error process took place before this seven-color spectrum was established as red–orange–yellow–green–blue–indigo–violet. Color scholar Ogata Koji surveyed the nomenclature variations of the seven rainbow colors in Japanese and found several fluctuations, such as red and crimson; orange and citron; navy blue and indigo; and purple, wisteria,

Table 2.2   Categorization of a rainbow: English, Shona, and Bassa

English

Purple	Blue	Green	Yel-low	Orange	Red

Shona

cips^wuka	citema	cicena	cips^wuka

Bassa

hui	zĩza

Source Gleason, *An Introduction to Descriptive Linguistics* (1955)

and bellflower.[16] In the early Meiji period, a color science textbook for children, *Irozu Mondou*, clearly stated that the rainbow has seven colors.[17] This book translates British color science, taught in a Q&A format. The idea that the rainbow has seven colors spread through these teaching materials.

According to zoologist Toshitaka Hidaka's essay "How Many Colors Are in a Rainbow?", various countries have differing classifications of rainbows. For example, Americans categorize them as six colored, whereas Belgians categorize them as five. He was surprised to discover that Americans and Belgians didn't use the seven-color categorization for rainbows, despite the fact that he had learned that rainbows were made up of seven colors. He explained that categorizations can greatly impact communication, even if we are referring to the same thing.[18] Because of the Japanese tendency to believe textbooks as written, many people now assume it is common knowledge worldwide that a rainbow has seven colors. Still, as we have seen, the actual number of rainbow colors differs across countries.

Meanwhile, in England, the birthplace of Newton,[19] who was the first to write that the rainbow has seven colors, the "rainbow has six colors" school of thought seems to have gained some ground in recent years. In my Color Theory class, which is offered in English for international students, I said, "Newton began to call the rainbow seven colors, and in the United Kingdom and the United States, people remember the colors that make up a rainbow. In the UK and the United States, to remember the colors that make up the rainbow, we use the letters Roy G. Biv, which stands for red, orange, yellow, green, blue, indigo, and violet, just like the names of people." An international student from the UK said that in the UK, the seven colors are just Newton's wishful thinking, and blue and indigo are considered one group; classical English is starting to recognize that the rainbow has six colors. Nevertheless, despite the many theories regarding the number of colors a rainbow can have, no consensus has been reached.

[16] Ogata, K. (2001). "Color Names of the Rainbow." In *Color Forum JAPAN 2001*, edited by The Four Societies of Optics.

[17] Iehara, M. (1876). *Irozu Mondou.*

[18] Hidaka, T. (1984). *The Language of Dogs*, pp. 19–20.

[19] Sugiyama, K. (2013). A Picture History of the Rainbow, p. 156.

2.2 Newton's Rainbow Color Discovery Through Musical Comparison

Why did Newton choose seven? In 1665, with the Great Plague spreading in England, Newton was under quarantine at home because of the closure of Cambridge University, spending his time reading and experimenting at his parents' home in Woolthorpe, his hometown. During this stay, Newton accomplished all three major achievements in fundamental science (prisms in optics, universal gravitation in mechanics, and the proof of calculus in mathematics). After reading about Descartes' refraction optics, Kepler's optics, and Hooke's microphotographs, Newton became interested in the reflection and refraction of light. Whilst refining lenses, he discovered that white light passing through a triangular prism could be separated into many colors.

Newton has been called the last alchemist.[20] In Japanese, the term alchemist is associated with mysterious hermits who study to create precious metals from base metals. In the seventeenth century, when science as an academic discipline was borderless, alchemist meant any scientist who tried to create an immortality potion called the "philosopher's stone" or "elixir of life." Lens polishing may have led to Newton's discovery of the rainbow spectrum, through a trial-and-error process by shining light through some lenses.

Newton's experiment was as follows. Sunlight was directed into a dark room through a small hole, and a prism lens was placed in its path. A rainbow spectrum appeared on the wall when white light passed through it. In other words, sunlight consists of a mixture of colored light of different wavelengths, which becomes white when all of them are mixed. This experiment demonstrated spectroscopy and additive color mixing as the cornerstones of modern optics. Spectroscopy is the division of light containing various wavelengths into its wavelength components, while additive color mixing adds light to light to create color. This discovery overturned the common belief in Europe since ancient Greece that all colors were formed from the contact of black and white. Furthermore, Newton revealed that an object's color depends on the reflective properties of its surface through the irradiation of colored light, which is categorized by a prism, onto the object's surface separately. Since objects

---

[20] Newman, W. R. (2018). *Newton the Alchemist: Science, Enigma, and the Quest for Nature's "Secret Fire"*. Princeton University Press.

2 CATEGORIZING THE RAINBOW   25

have different reflectance and absorbance for each light, the object's color appears to change according to the color of the illuminated light.[21]

Although Newton has been credited with assigning seven colors to the rainbow, his writings make clear that he did not in fact regard these colors as absolute, since there was also an infinite variety of intermediate colors. In the Latin draft of *Optics* Newton described five colors, but changed it to seven in the English version, published later.[22] A possible reason for Newton's change of mind is that he was a keen student of the Bible and believed in Kabbalistic mystical philosophy, in which scientific predictions could be made from Biblical numbers and symbols.[23] It is becoming more common for historians of science to recognize that Newton's view of natural science is broadly linked to occult studies, numerology, and hermitic and alchemical worldviews. Seven is one of the perfect numbers according to Christianity, and the Bible mentions seven days a week, the seven seals in Revelation, the seven trumpets, and the seven bowls. Newton may have been trying to give the rainbow seven colors to give it legitimacy in the Christian world.

He also connected the number seven to the seven-note scale CDEFGAB which he arranged in a wheel shape. Taking a length equal to that of the visible spectrum on the outer extension of the red color and finding the ratio of the lengths from its end to the dividing line of each spectral color show that these are approximately proportional to the length of the strings of a stringed instrument, so he made the dividing line of the colors of the rainbow correspond to DEFGABC (the le–mi–fa–so–la–ti–do) of the scale.[24] The entire development of Newtonian color theory is tied to the ancient Greek Pythagoras's (582–496 BCE) worldview of scales and "music of the celestial spheres." The octave scale is the foundation of Western music, based on the Pythagorean temperament. The "music of the celestial spheres" is the idea that the Sun and each of the six planets Mercury, Venus, Earth, Mars, Jupiter, and Saturn play

---

[21] Newton. (1983). *Opticks* Japanese translation, pp. 65–68.

[22] Itakura, K. (2003). *Is the Rainbow Seven Colors or Six?—Thinking about the Problem of Truth and Education.*

[23] The Associated Press. (2007, June 19). "Papers Show Isaac Newton's Religious Side, Predict Date of Apocalypse."

[24] Newton. (1983). *Opticks* Japanese translation, pp. 150–154.

a scale of one octave, as detailed by the German astronomer Johannes Kepler (1571–1630) in *The Harmony of the Universe* (1619).[25]

In addition, Newton appears to have been inspired by Athanasius Kircher (1601–1680), a Jesuit monk, music theorist, and mathematician. Kircher propounded the theory that sound was in objective correspondence with specific colors.[26] In polyphony (polyphonic music, from *poly* = many, *phony* = sound), different melodies (soprano, alto, tenor, and bass) harmonize to produce music. Just as chords harmonize, multiple colors appear to do the same, so assuming they must be linked would be natural. In support of his predecessors' theories, it is understandable that Newton would be tempted to assert that the octave scale and the colors of the rainbow are correlated.

This theory and worldview, in which the seven colors of the rainbow correspond to a musical scale, inspired modern European colorists and artists, and simultaneously sparked debate. One of the leaders of such debate was the Jesuit monk and mathematician Louis Bertrand Castel (1688–1757), who published a paper titled "Optique des Couleurs" (1740) as a refutation of Newton's color theory. However, it was not highly regarded in the optical community due to its illogical content.[27]

However, what is interesting about Castel's achievement is his creation of the ocular harpsichord, an instrument that combines color and sound.[28] The ocular harpsichord is said to have had 60 small colored glass windows, each with a curtain that opened when the keyboard was struck. Castel considered the music of colors as if it resembled the universal language of all mankind in the Biblical period of Eden, a language lost during the construction of the Tower of Babel. He also claimed that even deaf audiences could enjoy music because of instruments that could "paint" sounds.[29] Castel's attempt to combine color and sound in an

---

[25] Kepler. (2009). *The Harmony of the Universe: An Enduring Cosmology*. Originally written in Latin, translated into Japanese, pp. 444–475. In the early twentieth century, some attempts were made to express the tones of the planets in music, as in Holst's suite *The Planets* (Op.32) (1914–1916).

[26] Cytowic, R. E. (2003). *The Man Who Tasted Shapes*.

[27] Schier, D. S. (1941). *Louis Bertrand Castel, Anti-Newtonian Scientist*.

[28] Hankins, T. (1994). "The Ocular Harpsichord of Louis-Bertrand Castel; Or, The Instrument That Wasn't," pp. 141–156.

[29] Peel, James. (2006). "The Scale and the Spectrum." *Cabinet*. Winter (22). Retrieved November 28, 2016. https://www.cabinetmagazine.org/issues/22/peel.php

instrument is interesting and deserves to be re-evaluated. However, in the caricature in Fig. 2.4, he is depicted as a suspicious figure playing an ocular harpsichord while covering his head with water to wake up a rainbow. In Europe during the Enlightenment in the late seventeenth and eighteenth centuries, which emphasized reason and objective verification, he was likely the subject of caricatures as a mysterious person who created a mysterious instrument.

The question of what colors are in a rainbow and why they are categorized leads to a discussion of whether a color is an objective physical phenomenon or a subjective experience that can exist because we can see

Fig. 2.4 A caricature of Louis-Bertrand Castel's ocular organ, Charles Germain de Saint Aubin (1721–1786) (*Source* Waddesdon, The Rothschild Collection [The National Trust])

it. Adopting a perspective different from Newton's Enlightenment experiment, the Romantic novelist, poet, lawyer, politician, and natural scientist Johann Wolfgang von Goethe (1749–1832) deepened the discussion on the relation between subjective color and music. In *Theory of Color*, Goethe compiled his studies of all color phenomena, from physiology to natural occurrences, works of art, and crafts. This major work, which took about 20 years to write, is the book that changed the Romantic and then Impressionist painters' awareness of color. In *Theory of Color*, Goethe quotes painter Johann Leonhard Hoffmann (c. 1740–1814) to introduce the correspondence between color and tone.

Indigo	cello
Ultramarine	viola and violin
Green	human voice
Yellow	clarinet[30]

Later, the Russian-born painter and art theorist Wassily Kandinsky (1866–1944), taught his Bauhaus students the correlation between color and music and wrote about it in his book, metaphorically describing the correspondence between color and musical instruments as follows:

Yellow	sharp sound of a trumpet blown high
Orange	tuba fanfare tone
Red	violin tone
Reddish purple	passionate mid-to-low cello tone
Purple	sound of an oboe or a reed flute
Dark purple	bassoon tone
Light blue	sound of a flute
Dark blue	cello, which resembles the sound of a double bass as it grows darker and deeper
Blue (sound)	bass part of a pipe organ
Green	the midrange tone of a violin played gently[31]

The relation between color and sound is only a subjective, relative sensation and therefore cannot be shared with others consistently

---

[30] Goethe, J.W. von (1810). *Theory of Colors (History)*.

[31] Kandinsky. (1912). *Concerning the Spiritual in Art*.

2   CATEGORIZING THE RAINBOW   29

and stably. For example, a violin is lapis lazuli to Hoffman and red to Kandinsky. Yellow was also described as the woodwind clarinet for Hoffman and the brass trumpet for Kandinsky. Some people, including Kandinsky, are called synesthetes (synesthesiasts). Synesthesia is when one stimulus triggers multiple sensations, including color and sound.

The emergence of modern art coincided with the rise of synesthesia, which popularized the idea of associating sound and color. I used Google Ngram Viewer to research "synesthesia (also spelled synaesthesia)." Interestingly, synesthesia has become a commonly used word in English since the end of the 19th century. However, synesthesia and synesthetes (synesthesiasts) likely existed worldwide long before the 19th century. Modern art creators consider musical visualization a popular source of inspiration. For example, French art movements of the early twentieth century, such as Orphism[32] and American Synchromism,[33] were inspired by the correlation between color and music to create abstractly expressed pictorial works.

The theory that the rainbow has seven colors and is associated with music spread throughout the world. The first Japanese physics book, *Kikai Kanran*[34] (1827), published about 150 years after Newton, describes how "a prism with three ridges refracts sunlight, projecting a spectrum of colors onto a paper. ...Comparing the angle of light rays with the musical scale reveals that color and sound operate on the same principle." The learning that the rainbow had seven colors and that color and music were correlated reached Japan through the Netherlands. During the Edo period, Japan only traded with the Netherlands, and Western scholarship was introduced only through Dutch scholars. However, it is important to remember that the human categorization of colors in a rainbow is subjective, despite the various theories about their number and range of colors from where to where.

[32] The term "orphism" is said to be an allusion to Orpheus, the master of the lyre in Greek mythology, and to the richness of the colors used by painters belonging to this trend, which evokes music.

[33] An American school of painting that abstractly uses color and sound. Stanton MacDonald-Wright and Morgan Russell are representative figures.

[34] *Kikai Kanran* (1827) (reprint 1978).

2.3 Natural Fine Categorization: The Fraunhofer Line

The dividing line that determines the number of colors in a rainbow exists both subjectively and as a physical phenomenon. These colors seem continuous, but when the actual rainbow is magnified, it is categorized not by seven but by 10,000 units of natural fine barcode-like black lines. Fraunhofer lines are illustrated by the French colorist Chevreul in his mid-nineteenth-century book *Colours and their application to the industrial arts, using chromatic* circles (see Fig. 2.5). The term "solar spectrum" refers to the rainbow band of colors of visible light after it has passed through the prism. When this spectrum is magnified, the Fraunhofer lines can be observed. The Sun and other stars emit light at all wavelengths. When light passes through gases such as oxygen, sodium, calcium, and iron in the Sun's atmosphere, wavelengths that correspond to the parts of these gaseous elements are absorbed. Because light is absorbed rather than reflected, a black line appears on the wavelength portion of the spectrum.[35] Fraunhofer lines are named after the German optical instrument maker and physicist Joseph von Fraunhofer (1787–1826), who built a prism spectrograph in 1813 and discovered more than 500 of these black lines the following year. Table 2.3 displays the typical Fraunhofer lines, their associated elements, and wavelengths labeled with musical code-like alphabets.

However, it is impossible to see Fraunhofer lines in a rainbow in the sky with the naked eye, so anyone who wants to observe them must use a prism to disperse and project the light refracted from sunlight. About 25,000 Fraunhofer lines in the spectrum above the wavelength of 2950 Angstroms (Å) to 10,000 Å[36] have now been found.

The number of colors of the rainbow, where it should be divided and into what colors varies across cultures and languages and is not strictly fixed. Besides, if one wanted to separate these colors chemically, one would have to subdivide them into 10,000 units. The rainbow is the pinnacle of the myriad ways of dividing colors. I will continue to explore

---

[35] Yamamoto, S. (2001). "Separating Signals from Space," University of Tokyo Sogo Kenkyukai (Ed.). (2001). Dividing. pp. 107–109.

[36] One Angstrom is equivalent to 10^{-8} cm.

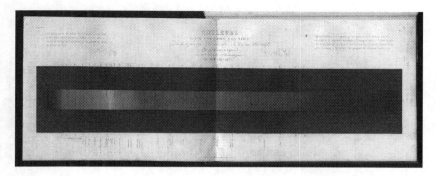

Fig. 2.5 Chevreul, M. E. (Michel Eugène) (1864). "Plate I: Couleurs d'Un Spectre Solaire." In Des Couleurs Et De Leurs Applications Aux Arts Industriels à l'Aide Des Cercles Chromatiques. Paris, France: J.-B. Baillière et fils

Table 2.3 List of typical elements and wavelengths of Fraunhofer lines

Fraunhofer lines	Chemical element	Wavelength (nm)
A	Oxygen O_2	759.370
B	Oxygen O_2	686.719
C	Balmer series hydrogen H-alpha	656.281
D_1	Sodium Na	589.594
D_2	Sodium Na	588.997
D_3	Helium He	587.565
E_2	Iron Fe	527.039
F	Hydrogen H	486.134
G	Iron Fe	430.790
H	Calcium ion Ca^+	396.847
K	Calcium ion Ca^+	393.368

the phenomenon of the rainbow and how many colors we can see in the world, how we divide them, and what names we assign to the categorized parts.

2.4 The Rainbow Flag

The acronym LGBT (lesbian, gay, bisexual, and transgender), refers to sexual minorities; in some cases, LGBTQ+ is used, which includes "queer," a generic term for such minorities. Sexual minorities suffer from human rights issues, such as difficulty in expressing their sexual orientation, being prohibited from marrying the person they want to, being disadvantaged in employment, being subjected to ridicule and violence, and the inability to choose their own clothing.

After the Stonewall Rebellion, a riot against police officers at the Stonewall Inn, a gay bar in Greenwich Village, New York, on June 28, 1969, the gay liberation movement flourished, and LGBTQ+ parades became popular in many urban areas in the US and Europe. June, the month in which the Stonewall Rebellion took place, is designated as Pride Month for the LGBTQ+ community.

The six-color rainbow flag is a well-known LGBTQ+ symbol created by artist Gilbert Baker (1951–2017). While serving in the US Army in San Francisco, Baker met gay politician Harvey Milk (1930–1978) and began working with him in his human rights activities.[37] Baker was himself a homosexual and drag queen, and it was at Baker's suggestion that the rainbow flag was first raised in a mass parade in San Francisco on June 25, 1978, to protest the unequal treatment of and laws against LGBT people. Baker describes the meaning of the rainbow flag as follows:

> *The rainbow is a part of nature, and you have to be in the right place to see it. It's beautiful, all of the colors, even the colors you can't see. That really fit us as a people because we are all of the colors. Our sexuality is all of the colors. We are all the genders, races, and ages.*

At first, Baker did not expect the rainbow flag's popularity to spread worldwide. The struggle for LGBTQ+ social status under this flag continued long after 1978.[38] Harvey Milk, along with the mayor of San Francisco, was assassinated by Daniel James White (1946–1985) on November 27, 1978. The biopic *Milk* (2008) shows a scene in which a rainbow flag is raised. On June 26, 2005, 37 years after the 1978 parade,

---

[37] Sanders, R., & Salerno, S. (2018). *Pride: The Story of Harvey Milk and the Rainbow Flag*. Random House Books for Young Readers.

[38] Baker, G. (2019). *Rainbow Warrior: My Life in Color*. Chicago Review Press.

the US Supreme Court finally recognized gay marriage as a right guaranteed by the Constitution. The rainbow flag was included in the Museum of Modern Art (MoMA) collection in New York that same year.

With its various colors, the rainbow flag is known as a symbol of diversity and is used by many people worldwide. Initially, the rainbow flag had eight colors (hot pink, red, orange, yellow, green, turquoise, indigo, and purple). However, only six colors (red, orange, yellow, green, blue, and purple) are firmly established because of production issues. In 2004, the pictogram 🏳️‍🌈 was registered in Emoji 4.0 as a rainbow flag or pride flag.

Just as the rainbow can be categorized into two or three colors, or even 25,000 colors according to the Fraunhofer line, the most crucial factor is the diversity of human beings. I learned in Thailand that humans are not simply two poles, that is, sexual majority versus minority (LGBTQ+). Thailand, where gender diversity is quite advanced, has terms for 18 different genders. For example, a *tom* is a woman who dresses as a man and likes to be either a woman or a *dee*. A *dee* is a masculine woman or a woman who likes *toms*. My laboratory organizes a joint annual workshop with a Thai university to create digital art. When I observed the people working in restaurants and shopping centers in Bangkok and the teachers at the university, I often wondered which of the 18 genders they identified as. I have found society much freer in Thailand than in the United States, Europe, Japan, and other Asian countries. Thailand allows individuals to live in their preferred gender and clothing.

CHAPTER 3

Categorizing Colors by Name

*The colors were practically indistinguishable, and yet, especially when they were given names, there **was** a difference.*
Sheena Iyengar, *The Art of Choosing*, Chapter Five

Iyengar,[1] a social psychologist known for her book *Art of Choosing*, conducted the following color experiment. When containers of two similar colors of nail polish were given different names—Adore-A-Ball and Ballet Slippers—female students were asked to choose one. Many preferred Ballet Slippers, and said it looked more vibrant than Adore-A-Ball. Moreover, when the students were asked to choose by name without being shown the actual nail enamel, Ballet Slippers was the most popular choice. By contrast, when the participants were shown only the alphabetical symbols A (containing Adore-A-Ball) and B (containing Ballet Slippers) and the actual nail enamel, they responded that A (containing Adore-A-Ball) looked brighter and chose A more than B. In other words, the preference for nail enamels without names was reversed.

How colors look to humans may change according to their names. The results of an experiment where the preference of unnamed and named nail enamels with the same content was reversed demonstrate that

---

[1] She is well known for researching sampling jam varieties in supermarkets. She was also involved in research on color selection, although she has acquired blindness.

© The Author(s), under exclusive license to Springer Nature Switzerland AG 2024
K. Hidaka, *The Art of Color Categorization*,
https://doi.org/10.1007/978-3-031-47690-7_3

naming can influence choice when choosing between two similar colors. The same color may be perceived differently depending on whether its name is, for example, "fuchsia" or "magenta." Whether human perception and categorization of color originate from how humans see (color vision and brain judgment), or the name (language and cultural practices) remains unknown, but vision and language are intricately intertwined. This mystery has been discussed in psychology, physiology, linguistics, and informatics. Nevertheless, distinguishing colors by naming them is the first taxonomy that humans can easily understand.

3.1   Basic Color Terms: Their Universality and Evolution

The Japanese Industrial Standards (JIS) have categorized color names into three groups:

1. Conventional color names
2. Systematic color names
3. Basic color names[2]

JIS Z 8102: 2001 "Names of non-luminous object colours" is defined as follows.

4. The main terms used in this standard are defined based on JIS Z 8105 and other sources.

  a. >Systematic Color names that systematically categorize object colors.
  b. Conventional color names are customary expressions of identifying colors.

5. Classification of color names is distinguished as follows:

  5.1. Systematic color names
    a. Systematic color names for chromatic colors
    b. Systematic color names for achromatic colors
  5.2. Conventional color names

---

[2] The Color Science Association of Japan.(Eds.). (2006). Color in Life. In Color Science Course 2 (pp. 156–162).

3 CATEGORIZING COLORS BY NAME 37

6. Systematic color names include 6. Basic color names and their modifiers.
7. Basic color names

    7.1. Basic color names for chromatic colors are (red, yellow red or orange, yellow, yellow green, green, blue green, blue, purple blue or violet, purple, red purple).[3]

1. A conventional color name is, for example, rose, and ivory. Conventional color names produce significantly different results depending on the person who thinks of the color. This phenomenon occurs because conventional color names can easily be associated with local dyes, foods, animals, and other day-to-day objects. In summary, anything can be a color name. The color I think of when I hear the word "lavender" may differ from the color that others think of as lavender. Among conventional color names, colors culturally or officially typical of a particular country, such as crimson, pale blue, and royal blue, are sometimes grouped under traditional colors.

2. Systematic color names are a genre of color names in which basic color names such as red, yellow, green, and blue are preceded by modifiers such as "light" and "vivid" to facilitate the common recognition of a range of colors. The suffix "ish" can be added (e.g., grayish, blackish, and reddish). Although it is difficult to specify colors strictly, they are generally effective for conversational communication. It may be difficult to identify the difference between systematic color names and basic color names.

3 Basic color names are strictly limited to color names that almost all speakers of a language can commonly understand. Color names comprising a single lexical element are defined as "Basic Color Terms" (BCTs). Some researchers define a BCT as a color term that is limited to color names commonly understood by almost all speakers of a language and containing one lexical element.

We begin by examining the origins and development of (3), basic color names. In academic circles of linguistics, sociology, and cultural anthropology in the 1960s, cultural (linguistic) relativism was influential. It was an established theory that language profoundly influences our

---

[3] JIS Z 8102: 2001 "Names of non-luminous object colours".

38   K. HIDAKA

perception of colors, and every individual has a distinct way of interpreting them. Cultural relativism was proposed by anthropologist Franz Boas (1858–1942) in 1887 as a standard for anthropological research and was popularized by Boas's students. Based on this cultural relativism, the theory that color naming systems must also vary by language (linguistic relativism) was proposed by American linguists Edward Sapir (1884–1934) and Benjamin Lee Whorf (1897–1941). This idea became mainstream in linguistic and cultural anthropology in the first half of the twentieth century. Extreme linguistic relativism was the attitude that speakers of different languages perceive things differently and therefore cannot share a common understanding in language.

The prevailing logic of cultural relativism was that Western societies and other cultures could not share a common understanding and that these cultures therefore evolved to different levels. Extreme cultural relativists used the keyword "evolution" to divide human languages and cultures into socially evolved and non-evolved ones. This theory of evolution applies social Darwinism, popular from the 19th to early twentieth century, to human language and culture. In confluence with evolutionary theory, extreme linguistic relativism had instilled in academia a view of progress and retardation. Conversely, nowadays, the social Darwinism element has been removed, and linguistic relativism is respected as a theoretical support for diversity and multicultural conviviality (see Chapter 8, Sect. 8.3.3).

The psychologist Eric Heinz Lenneberg (1921–1975) and his colleagues were the first to question the view that speakers of different languages cannot share a common perception. In 1956 they conducted a color term study in English and Zuni[4] using a color chart[5] published by Munsell Color Company as a color stimulus. A color chart is a physical tool for accurately designating and distinguishing colors. *Kojien*'s (6th edition, the most authoritative dictionary of Japanese) definition is as follows: "A chart in which color samples are arranged systematically."[6] Lenneberg et al. asked informants to name as many color words as they could think of and then asked where the range of those colors was on

---

[4] Zuni is a language spoken in parts of New Mexico and Arizona in the United States.

[5] The Munsell Color Chart is based on the three attributes (hue, lightness, and saturation) popularized by Albert Munsell and was the standard color chart for the United States in the twentieth century.

[6] "Color [colo(u)r]," *Kojien* (6th ed.), 2008.

3 CATEGORIZING COLORS BY NAME   39

the color chart. The result was a list of 52 color words familiar to Zuni speakers.[7]

This study revealed a correlation: English and Zuni share that easily recognized (salient) colors are more likely to have a color name than those that are not easily recognized. In addition, while Zuni-only speakers do not usually separate orange and yellow as different colors, bilingual speakers of English and Zuni tend to distinguish orange as a different color from yellow.[8] Notably, yellow and orange color names exist in Zuni, but both are metaphorical terms for objects.

> *je: lhupziqananne* (Zuni) = yellow (literally, like yellow ochre) (English)
> */olenshinanne* (Zuni) = orange (literally, like the orange) (English)

The results of the study, which found that English and Zuni color names were translatable to each other, raised the following questions regarding Sapir and Whorf's linguistic relativism: Despite differences in the number of color names used, when we look at the same color chart, don't we want to name the colors that stand out the same way?

Inspired by the research of Lenneberg and others, a group of young scholars seeking to challenge and disprove extreme linguistic relativism published *Basic Color Terms: Their Universality and Evolution* (Berlin & Kay, 1969).[9] Brent Berlin, a cultural anthropologist, and Paul Kay, a linguist from the University of California, Berkeley, led a cross-cultural study on color naming. Their survey showed that color names in other languages can be roughly translated. Berlin and Kay's research was based on the question of whether the concept of "translatability" contradicts the idea of linguistic relativism, which suggests that the emergence of language is random and has no similarities with other languages. For instance, when an English speaker translates the Japanese word *aka* (red) as "red," it implies that there exists a universal category of color in both Japanese and English. Thus, an English speaker can comprehend what color a Japanese speaker is referring to.

Berlin and Kay's research is an interdisciplinary study that includes two elements from cultural anthropology and linguistics: (1) focal color and

---

[7] Lenneberg and Roberts (1956), *The Language of Experience: A Study in Methodology.*

[8] Lenneberg and Roberts (1956), pp. 30–32.

[9] Berlin, B., & Kay, P. (1969). *Basic Color Terms: Their Universality and Evolution.* University of California Press. Translated into Japanese by Kyoko Hidaka (2016).

40   K. HIDAKA

boundaries experiment with 20 language informants; and (2) language analysis and evolution based on literature and interviews in 98 languages. Initially derived from the experiment in (1), the study began with a linguistic investigation of how focal colors are named. While investigating various languages, Kay and his colleagues observed that some had many color terms while others had few. They hypothesized that there might be a pattern in the way color terms increase. As a result, the spin-off study (2) was conducted to systemize the increase in Basic Color Terms (BCTs).

1. *Focal color and boundaries experiment.* As part of their fieldwork in cultural anthropology, Berlin and his colleagues conducted a study on color categories by presenting color charts to participants and asking them to identify the focal color (the color they perceive as typical of a color on a color chart) and the range of colors (the boundaries of the area represented by the color name). The 20-language survey revealed that all ethnic groups identified similar areas on the color chart as the focal color, and drawing the boundary line for the color category was challenging for all. Only the Tzeltal speakers, whom Berlin specialized in surveying, had a sample size of 40 informants. Conversely, most informants from speakers of other languages had only one or two informants.

2. *Language analysis and evolution based on literature and interviews in 98 languages.* From a linguistic perspective, this study examines how color is linguistically classified. Kay and his colleagues used internal reconstruction from the literature and information from fieldworkers.[10] The process of internal reconstruction entails utilizing our comprehension of language evolution to reconstruct the history of language.

For the purposes of this study, Berlin and Kay first defined a BCT as a term that fulfills all four of the following conditions:

---

[10] Although only two principal researchers, Berlin and Kay, are well known, many individuals were involved in the research, including students and faculty members of the Anthropology and Linguistics Seminar at the University of California, Berkeley. For example, Haruo Aoki, a linguistics researcher at the University of California, Berkeley, provided Berlin and Kay with information on the color terms of the Nez Perce, a Native American tribe.

3 CATEGORIZING COLORS BY NAME   41

1. Comprises a single lexical element: monolexemic. In other words, it is not divided into a sentence or two or more parts.
2. Other color terms cannot be substituted for it (e.g., crimson, scarlet).
3. The range of objects to be described using that color term is very limited. For example, blonde is limited to skin or hair color: "blonde hair" but not "blonde tea."
4. It must be psychologically salient and conspicuous for informants.

Two conclusions were drawn from the study. First, humans transcend language and perceive the same focal colors on a color chart, such as white, black, and red. Second, the words that should be called BCTs are white, black, red, yellow, green, blue, brown, purple, orange, pink, and gray. In their work, Berlin and Kay referred to a phenomenon as "evolution," which I prefer to call an "increase." For a further explanation of this terminology, see Sects. 3.6 and 3.7.

Berlin and Kay's most outstanding achievement was their comparative investigation of the following: humans on Earth generally see and name colors similarly, based on multiple languages. The BCT study, which began with the Sapir–Whorf hypothesis—the disproof of linguistic relativism—led to Berlin and Kay's proof of the universality of color categorization across languages. Inspired by Berlin and Kay, cultural anthropology, linguistics, psychology, ophthalmology, brain science, education, and Egyptian archaeology[11] began to publish related studies. The debate on linguistic relativism vs. cultural universals occurred across various academic fields.

3.2   BOUNDARIES OF COLOR CHARTS

The 1969 evolutionary model has yet to be settled. It has been debated and revised by many scholars. In their focal color and boundaries experiment with informants of 20 languages, Berlin and Kay described the

---

[11] Baines, J. (1985). Color Terminology and Color Classification: Ancient Egyptian Color Terminology and Polychromy. pp. 282–297. Research conducted by Baines at Oxford University has revealed that the Ancient Egyptian language has four fundamental color terms, seven colors for paintings, and an additional nine color variations as the Egyptian civilization developed. The study suggests that this aligns with stages IIIa, V, and VII (incomplete) of Berlin & Kay's evolutionary model.

42   K. HIDAKA

difficulty the informants had in drawing the boundaries of the color categories on the color chart. As a supplement to the problem of subjects' confusion regarding drawing color lines, Kay and McDaniel, a linguist specializing in semantics, co-authored a paper entitled "Color Categories as Fuzzy Sets" (1975).[12] As an illustration of fuzzy sets, the paper compares two examples, "members of Congress" and "gourmets." The set category of "members of Congress" is a crisp set in which there are two choices: either Congressman or not. On the other hand, the group of "gourmets" is made up of individuals with varying levels of gourmetness. Unlike the term "Congressman," which is clearly defined, it is difficult to categorize someone as a gourmet or not. The degree of belonging to the group can be expressed through a membership function, which is used to represent ambiguous quantities in fuzzy inference. For instance, "Person A is more gourmet than Person B."

The paper explains that, similar to "gourmets," a set of colors (group or category) is a category that has no clear boundaries and cannot be divided—for example, "blue from this boundary and green on this side"—and may contain multiple focal colors. Biggam argues that a distinction should be made between the nomenclature of a basic color term and giving a primary color a category (Basic Color Categories, BCC).[13] The question remains whether naming and categorizing are two completely different acts.

Let's delve into the concept of boundaries in detail. A threshold is a value that separates one category from another, serving as the boundary of a conditional branch. The color spectrum of a rainbow exhibits a gradual change in hues, such as the transition from red to orange or blue to purple. Although Fraunhofer lines segment the spectrum into barcodes, no discernible sign or boundary distinguishes between the "red area" and the "orange area." Japanese astronaut Mamoru Mohri once remarked that he couldn't observe any borderlines on continents from space. Similarly, the borders or boundaries drawn on the spectrum can be considered color space. Kay and McDaniel carried out calculations to determine the normal distribution of each BCT on the spectrum. They showed the seven stages as a proposed correction to the evolutionary model of color terms (1975).

---

[12] Kay, P., & McDaniel, C. K. (1975). Color Categories as Fuzzy Sets. https://eric.ed.gov/?id=ED138093 (Accessed: 2021-05-10).

[13] Biggam, C. (2012). *The Semantics of Colour: A Historical Approach*. 6.5 "The role of the Hering primaries".

3 CATEGORIZING COLORS BY NAME   43

Among the corrections made in the 1975 model, the following two representative points are notable. First, the first stage, which in the 1969 evolutionary model was supposed to begin with only white and black, is now "either white, or red, or yellow" and "black, or green, or blue." This proposed correction would be consistent with the increasing number of color words in Japanese. A commonly held belief is that that the earliest BCTs in Japan were the four colors white, black, red, and blue, which are said to derive from the Japanese words manifest, dark, light, and vague, respectively.[14] Second, mixing colors to make other colors was introduced. This concept excluded brown, pink, purple, orange, and gray from BCT as mixed colors. For example, brown is a mixture of yellow and black, and pink is a bright red with white added. Furthermore, light blue should be incorporated as modified blue if pink remained a BCT.

After Berlin and Kay's research, Maffi,[15] Merrifield, and Cook co-authored *the World Color Survey* (2009),[16] which added 110 new languages to the 98 languages in *Basic Color Terms*. Notably, in the evolutionary model of color terms in 2009, BCTs have been consolidated into six colors: white, red, yellow, green, blue, and black. Here, there are five stages of increasing color names. The concept that BCTs are psychologically primary or pure colors, discussed in this chapter, has confirmed that there are only six BCTs.

The pre-drawn boundaries on the Munsell color chart used by Berlin and Kay were artificially drawn as a guide or scale for convenience. The chart was a ready-made product with two-dimensional (flat) paper on which the colors were divided by ruled lines. These lines were created to make it easier to distinguish between different colors. These borders were created from Munsell's (Albert Henry Munsell, 1858–1918; Munsell is discussed in detail in Chapter 4) idea of representing colors on a globe in the same way that latitude and longitude represent locations on a globe. The color gradations in the Munsell color chart are divided so that the steps away from the "medium brightness and vividness green (5G 5/5)," the standard color determined by Munsell, appear equally

---

[14] Maeda, U. (1980). *Color: Dye and Color.* p. 26.

[15] Terra Lingua, a non-profit organization for networking and policy promotion for biocultural diversity.

[16] Kay, P., Berlin, B., Maffi, L., Merrifield, W. R., & Cook, R. (2009). *The World Color Survey*.

44   K. HIDAKA

divided in perceptual terms. The three parameters of hue, value (lightness), and chroma (saturation) have three dimensions. However, the Munsell color chart maps the two dimensions like a map of Mercator projection, with the maximum saturation mapped to a two-dimensional paper. Both Lenneberg et al. and Berlin and Kay employed this type of color chart. As per the colorist Akira Kitabatake, the Munsell color chart is a two-dimensional representation of maximum saturation, as if it were the skin of a 3D color sphere. This means that a two-dimensional color chart cannot represent all colors of a three-dimensional solid such as a globe. The chart is inclined towards vivid colors, and the "focal color" is the most strikingly vibrant color on the chart. Simply put, the chart only represents the most saturated colors and not all colors.

Moreover, the first edition of Berlin & Kay's *Basic Color Terms* (1969, University of California Press) and the reprint (1999, Center for the Study of Language and Information) have different appendix color charts. This is because the Munsell Color Company, which existed until the 1970s, ended its color chart development after the Munsell Foundation donated its materials to the Rochester Institute of Technology in 1983.

In terms of appearance, there is a noticeable difference between the Munsell color chart of the first edition (Fig. 3.1) and the one created by Hale Color Consultants in 1999 (Fig. 3.2). The former has a white background, while the latter has a gray background, with numbers on the horizontal axis and the alphabet on the vertical axis. Additionally, the hue changes on the chart by Hale Color Consultants appear abrupt and rough. The change from a white background to a gray background may have reduced the shadow of the Hermann grid illusion (the illusion of fuzzy black dots on a white background between the grids). This experimental method utilizes pre-classified color chart products but has limitations and drawbacks. It is impossible to find cases where the criteria for color categorization fundamentally differ from those of the Munsell color chart (see Chapter 5 for the color categories of the Hanunóo tribe).

On the other hand, there is an alternative experimental approach to distributing color charts. It involves showing individual chips of pre-divided color charts and asking participants to explain how they should be grouped. Researchers can then ask about the criteria used to divide the colors into panels, such as which colors belong to which color name group. However, this method also has a limitation. Determining where to draw the boundary line can be challenging when dealing with gradated colors in previously disjointed chips.

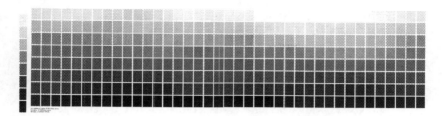

Fig. 3.1 Color chart by Munsell Color Company attached in supplement of Basic Color Terms (1969) (*Source* Munsell Color Company)

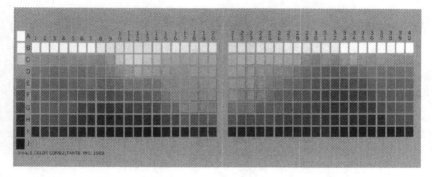

Fig. 3.2 Color chart by Hale Color Consultant attached in supplement of Basic Color Terms (1999) (*Source* HALE COLOR CONSULTANTS,INC 1989)

An experiment was conducted to test where the boundary line is found by dividing the frames into chips. Ichiro Kuriki et al., researching the brain mechanisms of visual perception, conducted a color category experiment on 57 Japanese speakers. The participants were shown each chip of a Munsell color chart separately and asked to respond with the color name; the parts of the color they recognized as different color categories were detected from the simultaneously measured brainwave activity. The results showed that Japanese speakers had 19 color name categories in common and that the brainwaves changed in 11 color categories. Notably, the results corresponded to the 11 BCTs proposed by Berlin and Kay in 1969, and the brainwaves showed a response when the focal color and its range were changed.

46   K. HIDAKA

The color chart used by Kuriki et al. before dividing it into discrete chips is very similar to the Hale Color Consultants' color chart from the 1999 edition. The Hale Color Consultants' chart has a steeper change in hue than the Munsell color chart from the 1969 edition.

To ensure accurate color categorization, the experiment's designer established specific guidelines. These guidelines included which manufacturer's color chart to use, how the colors should be arranged, and whether they should be grouped together or separated into distinct chips. It's worth noting that these guidelines were not set in stone and were subject to some degree of flexibility.

3.3   Color Charts and Lighting

Colors exist, but they cannot be perceived without a source of light. Additionally, light itself can have color and can influence how an object appears. Let us explore the link between the color chart and experiment lighting.

Environmental lighting has a significant impact on the appearance of color. The property by which a lighting source affects how an object's colors appear is called a "color rendering." Objects viewed under a light source similar to sunlight appear to have more natural colors than those viewed under artificial light. However, real sunlight changes direction and color with time and season. In printing color proofing, or in places where color appearance is crucial, such as beauty salons or clothing retailers, it is desirable to use lamps with improved color rendering. For example, for color-proofing photographs, using a light source with a color temperature of 5000 K is desirable.

The use of reddish light for the lighting when Berlin and Kay showed the Munsell color chart to their subjects was another factor that could have biased their judgment. A note in *Basic Color Terms* (1969) specifies that the ambient lighting when the color chart was shown was "a high intensity lamp #1133" bulb with a color temperature of 2900 Kelvin and an output of "Low."[17] It further states that this ambient light was "close to the International Commission on Illumination's standard light source." The International Commission defined a standard light source

---

[17] Berlin, B., & Kay, P. (1969). p.161.

on Illumination[18] in 1931 as A, B, and C: the A light source is a gas-filled tungsten incandescent bulb with a color temperature of 2854 Kelvin, and the B and C light sources have color temperatures of 4870 Kelvin (average noon sunlight) and 6840 Kelvin (daylight), respectively, where Kelvin corresponds to the color temperature (light color) unit. However, only Berlin, for some reason, showed the color chart to 40 Tzeltal informants under sunlight. The reason for this decision is not recorded in the book and remains unclear. I suspect that the Tzeltal insisted on seeing the colors in sunlight. In any case, the Tzeltal were subjected to a different environment, and possibly, the subjects saw the same color chart differently under incandescent lamps and under sunlight, even if they were provided with the exact instructions. For example, under the 2900 Kelvin lamp in Berlin and Kay's experiment, yellow looks reddish, and green on the chart looks dull.

Sunlight contains wavelengths in the visible light range in approximately equal amounts. Still, incandescent lamps appear reddish because of their long-wavelength components, and red and orange objects appear somewhat dull under fluorescent lamps, which have few long-wavelength components. In addition, under sodium lamps, which produce monochromatic light of approximately 589 nanometers, objects other than orange objects appear grayish and dull.

Some stores intentionally use slightly pinkish fluorescent lights to make meat on the shelf look fresher, and the freshness of meat may differ when viewed off the shelf. Fluorescent lamps contain light with many green and blue wavelengths; thus, when red objects are illuminated, they appear dull, whereas blue objects appear bright. When a fluorescent lamp with pinkish light is shone on a red object, the object will appear bright and appealing, even if the same lamp is used for other objects. On the other hand, incandescent lamps contain light with yellowish and orange wavelengths, which makes blue objects appear dull. However, red objects become more vivid when illuminated by such lamps.

Although there are standard light sources, unifying the brightness and coloration of ambient light and lighting in experimental environments using color charts in various countries would take a lot of work. The color palette of van Gogh's paintings underwent significant changes depending on the environmental light of his location, with a marked

---

[18] Commission Internationale de l'Éclairage (CIE).

contrast between his time in Paris and Southern France and his time in the Netherlands. I am fascinated by the diversity, tastes, and cultural characteristics that emerge from regional differences, for example, differences in the color of pastries between Japan and New York. Still, this experiment may appear ambiguous for individuals who want absolute standards.

The lighting for viewing the Munsell color charts might have had a European preference bias. When I lived in the United States and the United Kingdom, I sensed that many people of European descent, especially Scandinavians, preferred the red lighting of incandescent bulbs (Fig. 3.3). Incandescent bulbs lit restaurants, houses, and libraries, but the illumination seemed much lower than in Japan. On Twitter, Sandra Haefelin (1975–), a half-German, half-Japanese author, mentioned that many Germans do not like the brightness of convenience store-like lighting:

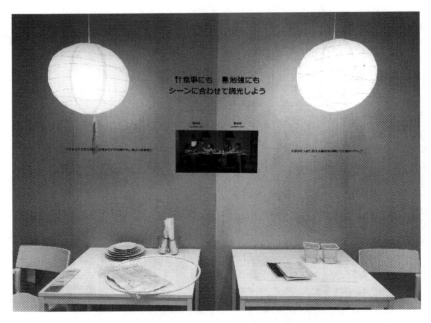

Fig. 3.3 Difference in color between incandescent and daylight white lighting (*Source* IKEA Tokyo-Bay)

3 CATEGORIZING COLORS BY NAME 49

Sandra Haefelin's tweet (now called X). @SandraHaefelin (May 29, 2020). They appear to be bothered by bright fluorescent lights🥴. Brightness, such as in a convenience store, is unsuitable for Germans.[19]

It is important to note that the use of LED bulbs has increased in many countries due to energy conservation awareness. It is also a fact that fewer people are familiar with the color of incandescent bulbs. A brightness and color temperature preference experiment on a set that does not like Japanese convenience store-like brightness and a set that likes Japanese convenience store-like brightness is necessary to advance the examination of color culture.

3.4 CATEGORIZING IN DETAIL

The categories of colors and human interest are discussed in this section.

The richness of the concept shows how close attention is paid to the properties of reality and how awake is the interest in the distinctions that can be introduced into it.[20]

Lévi-Strauss, *La Pensée Sauvage* (1962).

The renowned social anthropologist, Lévi-Strauss, founder of structuralism theory, explained the link between the development of conceptual vocabulary and human attention. It's easier to categorize colors based on their specific characteristics. In anthropology classes, the example of the Inuit people who live in snowy areas and have different words for various types of snow is often cited. However, if you grew up in a region with no snow, you wouldn't understand the analogy "Snow White is as white as snow" because you have never seen snow. For example, the reason there are many animal and food names in English color names is that animals and food are important to English speakers. The Japanese word for "cherry" means pinkish in color and is associated with the color of flowers, whereas the English word "cherry" refers to the color of reddish-purple fruits.

[19] Retrieved from https://twitter.com/SandraHaefelin/status/126629878178963 4566.

[20] Lévi-Strauss. (1976). *La Pensée Sauvage* (Japanese translation). p. 3.

The following two points are notable characteristics of Japanese customary and traditional color names. First, with few exceptions, such as rouge and vermilion, most color names are derived from plant dyes or the names of people or places. Second, colors, such as indigo and black, are named according to the stage of lightness and are subdivided. The most typical example is indigo dyeing, also known as Japan blue, which was used by ordinary people for everyday wear.[21] Table 3.1 shows that the gradation is divided into 22 levels with different color names, ranging from the lightest indigo white (*aijiro*) to the darkest navy (*noukon*).

However, these traditional color names have largely fallen out of use, and today only one or two color names are used colloquially for indigo. The Japanese language has many color names for blue hue groups: light blues are sky blue and pale blue, and dark blues are divided into indigo, navy blue, dark blue, and blue. However, Japanese light blue is not counted as a BCT because it is the name of a substance called water, and sky blue is the color of the sky.

Although not up to the Japanese indigo gradation, in Russian, the blue category is divided into two BCTs: light blue (*goluboy*) and dark blue (*siniy*). Few languages have more than two blue BCTs; thus, Russian is a special case. Russian has six words for shades of cyan alone, revealing a fascination with blue.[22] While English distinguishes pink and red as separate colors, Russian has historically differentiated between light and dark shades of blue. Biggam explains the difference between macro color terms (BCTs) and micro color names (finely divided, or names that refer to specifics).[23] However, both names indeed refer to blue for Russians.

Does a person's language affect how they categorize colors? Specifically, does a speaker's color category system impact their sorting of colors? In a 1994 study by Andrews, a Slavic linguist from Georgetown University, the blue color classification of Russian and other language speakers was analyzed. Four groups were tested: (1) Russians who came of age during the Soviet Union, (2) those who moved to Russia after coming of age, (3) those who moved to Russia as young adults, and (4) US

---

[21] Aizome, the "Mystical Japan Blue": *Tradition, Shopping, Products & Services.* https://japan-magazine.jnto.go.jp/en/1505_aizome.html (Accessed: Apr 24, 2021).

[22] https://www.quora.com/Why-does-the-Russian-language-have-two-names-for-the-color-blue (Ref. 2021-04-22) 'Why does Russian have two names for blue?'.

[23] Biggam, C. (2012). *The Semantics of Colour: A Historical Approach.* "3.6 Elicited lists".

3 CATEGORIZING COLORS BY NAME 51

Table 3.1 How Japanese indigo dyes are categorized by color names based on their lightness

Color names of indigo	Lightness
aijiro	
mihanada, mizuhanada	
kamenozoki	
mizuasagi	
asagi	
usuhanada	
usuai	
hanaasagi	
asahanada	
nando	
hanada	
tetsu	
noshime	
ai (literally, indigo)	
aisabi	
kon-ai	
aitetsu	
kachi	
shikon	
tomekon, tomarikon	
kachigaeshi	
noukon	

English speakers. The first three groups were tested in Russian, while the fourth was tested in English. The study found a difference in classification between monolinguals and bilinguals. Russian-only speakers continued to classify blue into two colors, whereas bilingual speakers of English and

52   K. HIDAKA

other languages learned to perceive blue as one large category. Based on these results, Andrews concluded that there are two blue BCTs in Russian. This experiment led to the theory that color names are not based on perception but on differences in the taxonomy of the languages used.[24]

Speakers of languages distinguishing between light and dark blue can perceive and differentiate between these colors more quickly than those without this distinction. It highlights the importance of language and how it can shape our perceptions and experiences of the world around us. Winawer et al.[25] conducted an experiment in which Russian speakers, who divide the color blue into two categories, and English speakers, who consider blue to be a single category, were asked to sort blue squares of different lightness into either light blue (*goluboy*) or dark blue (*siniy*), and the speed at which they could determine the boundary line was measured. For this experiment, 26 native Russian and 24 native English speakers were recruited in Boston. The study found that Russian and English speakers took longer to classify cards with colors close to the boundary area, specifically light blue and dark blue which were difficult to differentiate. However, native Russian speakers were more likely to quickly separate blue into two categories, while native English speakers tended to consider blue as a single category without separating it. Based on the difference in categorization speed, Winawer et al. concluded that native language influences color categorization.

Thus, how do bilingual speakers, people from different linguistic and cultural backgrounds, see and perceive color? Olga Loitšenko of the University of Tallinn, Estonia, studied the range of blue colors and linguistic representations of bilingual speakers in the neighboring countries of Russia and Estonia. Similar to Russian, Estonian has two color words for blue, *helesinine* (bright blue) and *sinine* (blue). There were four groups of participants, bilingual in Russian and Estonian. The first group was Estonian and speakers fluent in Estonian, and the second group was Estonian and speakers fluent in Russian. The third group comprised Russian speakers fluent in Estonian, and the fourth group comprised Russian speakers fluent in Russian.

---

[24] Andrews, D. (1994). The Russian Color Categories *Sinij* and *Goluboj*: An Experimental Analysis of Their Interpretation in the Standard and Emigré Languages. p. 10.

[25] Winawer, J., et al. (2007).

These four groups were asked where they would divide the color chart as *helsinine/goluboy* (bright blue) or *sinine/sinij* (blue). In the experiment to divide the color chart by color name, all groups responded with the same name to almost identical color chips. However, in an experiment to indicate which colors they felt stood out in the color chart, only the first group, Estonians with good Estonian language skills, felt that *sinine* (blue) stood out. By contrast, the remaining three groups, those with good Russian language skills and Russians, said that red stood out.[26]

Speakers of languages from neighboring countries give the same color names to the same colors in the same way, but the colors they find conspicuous differ. Estonia is a former communist country and a current member of NATO, and has had tense relations with the neighboring former Soviet Union. The Russian language originally recognized both blue and red as valuable colors. However, due to their political implications throughout history, the significance of these colors has shifted. In Russian pronunciation, the color red is associated with beauty and is a prominent symbol of communism. In ex-communist countries, especially Russia (former Soviet Union), the importance surrounding the color red may be heavier than for other colors. Although difficult to determine, a possibility is that in Russia and the other linguistic cultures that have experienced communist states, the color red may be perceived as more important and prominent than other colors.

In Hungarian, a language of a former communist state, similar to Russian blues, the red category has two BCTs, *piros* and *vörös*. The two types of red in Hungarian do not range by brightness or hue but by object or scene. *Piros* and *vörös* in Hungarian translate to "red" in Japanese, but studies show that the choice between the two varies by the scene and object of use.[27] Benczes and Tóth-Czifra, linguistics professors at the Institute of Communication and Sociology at Budapest Corvinus University, analyzed these two types of red from the Hungarian corpus (linguistic data). Despite the difference in brightness and degree of nuance between these two colors, they are both in the red category. According to Benczes and Tóth-Czifra, *piros* often refers to objects being red, whereas *vörös* is

---

[26] Loitšenko, O. (2018). Colour terms in the BLUE area among Estonian-Russian and Russian-Estonian bilinguals, pp. 285–299.

[27] Benczes, R., & Tóth-Czifra, E. (2014). "The Hungarian colour terms piros and vörös: A corpus and cognitive linguistic account." *Acta Linguistica Hungarica*, 61(2), pp. 123–152.

54   K. HIDAKA

more likely to be used figuratively.[28] They explain that *piros* is mainly used when clothes and man-made objects are red, and *vörös* is used for natural objects, for example, cabbage (Hungarian *vörös káposzta*), animal hair, and blood.

The cause of the detailed division of color names, even when referring to the same color, seems to be a combination of various factors, such as dyes and pigments used in a particular region, a commitment to a particular color, and the influence of political systems and other ideologies. Different countries and languages emphasize different things, leading to different ways of dividing colors.

3.5   PUTTING IT TOGETHER BROADLY

In this section we discuss the process of translating color names. An example is languages in which green and blue are grouped in the same word. Japanese speakers are familiar with referring to green as blue—because green apples are called 'blue' apples (*ao-ringo*), 'blue' vegetables (*ao-yasai*) and 'blue' traffic lights (*ao-shingo*). As discussed, Berlin and Kay first proposed BCT research because of translatability into English.[29] However, foreigners think it odd that the Japanese call traffic lights and apples blue instead of green. In *Basic Color Terms*, Japanese color terms are treated as a case of questionable evolutionary order.

In my experience in translation, color names, especially blue and green, are often not directly translated. In the original title of the famous picture book *The Very Hungry Caterpillar*, Caterpillar is translated as a blue worm (*ao-mushi*). Still, a green caterpillar is depicted on the cover and throughout the book. The green pepper (Fig. 3.4) is described as "fresh green chili" and the original Japanese says, "blue chili" (*ao-togarashi*). Stanlaw's paper further mentions the issue of blue traffic lights, explaining that blue is used in Japanese for traffic lights and "complexion." He also pointed out that blue means "just beginning, freshness."[30]

It is widely accepted across some languages that green is often categorized together with blue, providing a clear example of linguistic relativism.

---

[28] Ibid.

[29] Berlin, B., & Kay, P. (1969), p. 2.

[30] Stanlaw, J. (1997). Two Observations on Culture Contact and the Japanese Color Nomenclature System. p. 256. In C. Hardin & L. Maffi (Eds.), Color Categories in Thought and Language (pp. 240–260).

Fig. 3.4 Green chili peppers are packaged in English (fresh green chili peppers) and Japanese (ao togarashi), but the blue (ao) is not directly translated (*Source* Hidaka, K. [2017])

The confusion between green and blue is also mentioned in *Basic Color Terms* among speakers of Japanese, speakers of Tzeltal, a Mayan language of southern Mexico, and speakers of Tzotzil, a Mayan language belonging to the same group as Tzeltal. According to a survey, as of 2000, Tzeltal had approximately 140,000 speakers from Mexico to California.[31] Of the 40 Tzeltal speakers for whom Berlin collected data, 31 pointed to the focal color of *yaš* in the green area, and nine pointed to the blue area. Furthermore, a survey by anthropologist Collier, who provided information to Berlin and Kay, found that Tzotzil also equated green and blue. However, Spanish, Mexico's official language, separates green and blue as different colors. Hence, bilingual speakers of Spanish and Mayan do not equate green and blue.

From the perspective of modern English speakers, languages that call green and blue by the same name are intriguing. Kay and McDaniel (1975) hypothesized that these languages have a composite concept color

---

[31] México. Lenguas indígenas nacionales en riesgo de desaparición: Variantes lingüísticas por grado de riesgo. (2012) INALI.

56   K. HIDAKA

GRUE for green and blue to explain examples such as those in Japanese and Mayan languages. The word GRUE is portmanteau.[32]

However, one theory posits that GRUE is not a cognate only of the Japanese or Mayan peoples. Blue and green were possibly grouped together in Old English, as in Japanese and the Mayan language family. According to Biggam, a linguist specializing in Old English semantics, there was a portmanteau, *hæwen* (or *hæwen*, the spelling varies), in medieval English, referring to blue and green.[33] However, Old English *hæwen* was replaced by *bleu*, which came from French. Green and blue are completely separate categories in the 1960s English spoken by Berlin and Kay.

It is crucial to understand that the color categorizations in Celtic languages of the English-speaking world are not limited to the standard blue and green. The Celtic language group spoken in the United Kingdom, such as Gaelic in Scotland and Ireland, and Welsh, has a color term *glas* encompassing green and gray. Moreover, several commonly used English words such as "red" for hair color, onion, and cabbage cover a broad range of hues, ranging from orange to almost purple. Therefore, the color red includes a spectrum of adjacent hues.

In contrast to hair, onion, and cabbage, red and pink are the same hue, but English separates them into two independent words according to lightness. Pink was largely grouped as part of red. Berlin and Kay initially defined pink as a BCT, but pink was removed from primary BCTs in the revised evolution process.

As a Japanese speaker, if you ask me whether I perceive green and blue as one word like GRUE, the answer is no. I perceive green and blue as separate hues, each as a focal color. Following Japanese linguistic custom, I sometimes call green "blue" (*ao*), even though I perceive it as a different hue from blue. Despite recognizing blue and green as different colors, the Japanese still use blue for traffic lights. At the same time, Mayan languages identify blue and green as the same color, making it difficult to differentiate and translate GRUE.

Furthermore, the Japanese word for green (*midori*) is used to describe plants and trees, for example, "This city is full of green," which goes

---

[32] *Portmanteau*, French for a double-opening travel bag, is a word formed by adding two or more words. For example, brunch by adding breakfast and lunch, or frenemy by adding friend and enemy.

[33] Biggam, C. P. (1997). *Blue in Old English: An Interdisciplinary Semantic Study*.

beyond the definition of BCT in the narrow sense. Furthermore, there is a seemingly contradictory expression of Chinese origin, "green black hair,"[34] which, in the Japanese sense, refers to lush young hair. Although "green black hair" is an extreme example, figurative color words are also difficult to translate.

3.6 Increasing and Decreasing

Color vocabulary may differ across languages, even if they seem to have a limited number of color terms. Some languages have color names that do not have a direct equivalent in other languages, or that are no longer used. Unlike the theory of language universals by Berlin and Kay, which suggests that Basic Color Terms increase from few to many or from large categories to small ones, I believe that the number of color terms consolidates and decreases over time. Color names may be created, lost, or replaced by foreign loan words, and can expand and contract like the territory of a nation.

I would like to mention a rare case in which language universals do not apply. The Pirahã language, which is spoken deep in the Brazilian Amazon, possibly differs from the BCT evolutionary model of Berlin and Kay. Pirahã is a language in danger of disappearing, and at the time of the study, black, white, red (including yellow), and green (including blue) were BCTs. These BCTs correspond to Stage 3 according to Berlin and Kay's 1969 evolutionary model. However, an analysis of Pirahã color words determined that all BCTs are clauses if they are linguistically strictly literal transliterations. The structure to express black is "blood is dirty," for white "it is visible" or "it is transparent," for red "it is blood," and for green "immature at the moment."[35] The Pirahã people use sentences that compare colors to something. In other words, if Berlin and Kay's definition of BCT is applied, which takes color name as a single lexical element, it would correspond to the pre-BCT stage because there is no single-color name. The Pirahã unique worldview finds expression in its language, which lacks past- or future-tense concepts and only has two

[34] This expression appears in the poem "Qiu Xing" by Lu Yu (1125–1209), a poet of the Southern Song Dynasty. It is said that by sighing, his young black hair turned gray overnight.

[35] Everett (2012). *Don't Sleep, There Are Snakes: Life and Language in the Amazonian Jungle* (Japanese translation). pp. 169–170.

58   K. HIDAKA

numbers. This makes it an ideal case study for Sapir–Whorf linguistic relativism advocates.

Everett, who conducted the linguistic analysis of the Pirahã language, initially continued his research as a Christian missionary living in a Pirahã settlement. Inspired by the values of the Pirahã people, he later left missionary work. In Tokyo, I read the promotional message of Everett's book in the Japanese edition of *Don't Sleep, There Are Snakes: Life and Language in the Amazonian Jungle*. It stated, "In the Pirahã culture, there is no concept of right/left, no concept of numbers, and not even names for colors." I read that and wondered if it was true: is there really a language that doesn't have words for colors? I was excited when I read the Pirahãs' question, "Is your skin black like ours or white like yours?", which clearly shows that the Pirahã language is capable of recognizing differences in skin tone and discussing it with Everett. The Pirahã language may not fulfill the BCT criteria of Berlin and Kay, but it is a language that can express color and communicate with others. It was a bit misleading that the Pirahã language does not conform to Berlin and Kay's definition of a "lexical element." Upon reflection, I found the promotional message "Not even the names of colors" somewhat inaccurate.

It is unclear whether the Pirahãs had a way of expressing color before Everett arrived in the area. When living amongst people of the same language and race, unnecessary vocabulary may not be developed but can be triggered by association with people from outside. Words and concepts imported from other societies (foreign words) are used daily in modern society. For example, tsunami and sushi are used in English because general concepts unique to Japanese cannot be translated into English. The concept of "skin tone of a different race," previously unnecessary, may have entered the vocabulary. To increase the vocabulary of color terms, physical differences such as skin, hair, and eye color are used as a catalyst.

Although there may be an increase in new color expressions that may have originated from encounters between the Pirahã people and the white race, color words also increase artificially due to rivalry. In the first half of the twentieth century, there was a period when color-related organizations in the United States and the United Kingdom competed to mass produce English color names with national prestige. This period was from the 1920s to the 1930s, when the dominant force of American spelling[36] and pronunciation overtook that of British English. In 1930, McGraw-Hill Educational Press in the United States published Maerz and Paul's *A Dictionary of Color*,[37] a large treasury of English color names with approximately 3000 color names on 7056 color chips.[38] In 1931, the Inter-Society Color Council (ISCC) of the United States was established, and the ISCC-NBS color name encyclopedia comprised approximately 7500 color names.[39]

The spread of English color names by a US color dictionary could have been seen as challenging for those tasked with establishing the standard for British color terminology. Britain aimed to create a British version of the ISCC to compete with the United States. In 1931, The British Colour Council (BCC) was established as a color regulator and fashion information agency to "standardize the traditional colors of Britain." A color standards organization established with the strong nationalistic idea of determining traditional British colors and using them in national events, the BCC was actively engaged in publishing activities from its founding in 1931 to around the 1970s. The BCC also influenced Japan, and the foreign color names in *Color Standards* (1951) and *Dictionary of Color Names* (1954), published by the Japan Color Research Institute, were based on the color names of the BCC.[40]

The opposite situation, decreasing color words, should also be considered. Sometimes, color terms disappear due to the introduction of foreign words or loan words. In Japanese, many color names recorded in dictionaries and literary works are now obsolete. Okimori, who studies the history of color-word transition, writes that ancient Japanese color names were not called "XX-*iro*" (*iro* means color in Japanese) but, originally,

[36] For example, "color" is spelled "color" in American English but "colour" in British English, which indicates whether American or British English is currently the global standard.

[37] Maerz, A., & Paul, M. Rea. (1930). *A Dictionary of Color* (1st ed.). (2nd ed. 1950).

[38] *The New Handbook of Color Science* (3rd ed.). (2011), pp. 256; Fukuda, K. (1999). *Where Do the Names of Colors Come from—Their Meanings and Culture*, p. 31.

[39] The Color Science Asssociation of Japan (Ed.). (2006). *Color Science Course 2: Color in Life*, p. 162. NBS stands for the National Bureau of Standards, which existed until 1988. The organization changed its name and is now the National Institute of Standards and Technology (NIST).

[40] Sanzo Wada who was the founder of the Japan Color Research Institute, mentioned the British Color Council.

60   K. HIDAKA

"XX-*zome*" (*zome* or *some* means dye in Japanese).[41] The fact that ancient Japanese named colors based on dyes proves that dyers held the right to name colors. In the Heian period (794–1185), aristocratic women were involved in dyeing and wrote down numerous color names in their literary works. However, in everyday 21st-century speech, Japanese people do not use "XX-*zome*." Today in Japan, new creators of color names are not only in the fashion industry but also in product design, automobile manufacturing, the printing industry, and retail marketing, and many of these color names are foreign words.

Stanlaw, a linguistic anthropologist specializing in Japanese popular culture, conducted a generational survey of Japanese color vocabulary, including foreign color names, in the late 1990s.[42] In this survey, 91 Japanese speakers of various generations were asked to write down color names they considered important in their daily lives. Stanlaw translated the most frequent color names from white to rat into English, further indicating that gray and rat refer to the same color in Japanese. Dark blue to skin tone is also relatively common, and finally, dark brown to emerald green are categorized as less frequent but remain prevalent color words. Notably, the top four most frequent color words are white, black, red, and blue, which have been suggested as possible early BCTs. Stanlaw's findings and views are unlikely to be disputed by contemporary Japanese. According to Stanlaw, the following words are color names that appear in everyday Japanese conversations, which include many non-Japanese names: white, black, red, blue, yellow, green, brown, purple, pink, orange, gray (ash and rat), indigo, aqua blue, gold, silver, skin-color, dark brown, sky blue, pink, orange, gray, brown, khaki, beige, cream, lemon, emerald green.

Stanlaw drew two conclusions from his research. First, the Japanese language has close to 11 color names and focal colors that are included in Berlin and Kay's (1969) universal color-word model. It is also considerably influenced by loan words, particularly from English. Second, Stanlaw's study suggests that the Berlin and Kay model does not completely refute the theory of linguistic relativism proposed by Sapir–Whorf. In Japan, while green and blue are recognized separately, green

---

[41] Okimori, K. (2010). *A Historical Study of Color Language*. Oufu.

[42] Stanlaw, J. (1997). *Two Observations on Culture Contact and the Japanese Color Nomenclature System*, pp.240–260.

is often referred to as "blue" idiomatically, and Japanese uses many foreign, loan color words. This is not a universal color-word situation for humanity.

Since the Meiji era (1868–1912), Japan has had an influx of *katakana*[43] foreign loan words. Color names are no exception, and many have fallen into disuse in favor of foreign words. For example, orange, pink, gray, brown, and purple are foreign words (loan words), but in 21st-century Japan, these foreign words are used in daily life without question. For instance, to represent orange and pink, various color names derived from other fruits and flowers were originally used. Until the Edo period, there were traditional Japanese color names corresponding to these foreign words, but they are no longer used colloquially.

In addition, as of 2000, when asked what they called the color between black and white, 57% said "ash" and 7.2% said "rat," whereas approximately 20% of university students answered with the English loan word: "gray."[44] These data show that even color names considered relatively familiar, such as ash , are being replaced by gray in the colloquial language.

Thus, color names are increased or decreased by foreign words from other languages. This phenomenon of being surpassed by foreign words occurs not only in Japanese but also in other languages. For example, the Tagalog color blue in the Philippines was originally *bughaw*, but a loanword from Spanish, *asul* (originally spelled *azul* in Spanish), has also become common. This example exemplifies the use of a foreign or borrowed word in combination with an ancient traditional color name.

Furthermore, color words with cumbersome pronunciations are more likely to become obsolete because they require more effort than those that are not cumbersome. Henrich, an evolutionary biologist, explained that the three elements of language communication that are less likely to become obsolete are "complexity," "transmission efficiency," and "ease of learning," using color words and phoneme counts as examples.[45]

---

[43] *Katakana* is one of three writing systems (syllabary) used in Japanese, along with *hiragana* and *kanji*.

[44] Ono, A., et al. (2010). Investigation and Analysis of Color Vocabulary for the modern Japanese. *Journal of the Color Science Association of Japan*, 34(1), pp. 2–13.

[45] Henrich, J. (2016). *The Secret of Our Success: How Culture is Driving Human Evolution, Domesticating Our Species, and Making Us Smarter.* Princeton University Press. (Yasuko Imanishi, Trans.) (Hakuyosha, 2019), pp. 356–364.

62   K. HIDAKA

Conversation is spoken communication, and audibility and pronounceability are vital. In linguistics, there is a term called vowel harmony. In this phenomenon, the same vowel repeatedly appears in a word, for example, in words familiar to and frequently used by humans, such as *mimi* (ear) and *hoho* (cheek), which are body parts. Vowel harmony is said to result from reduced effort in pronouncing a language.

In my opinion, the reason why the Japanese language commonly groups blue and green together is because it is easier to pronounce *ao-ringo* (literally, blue apple) or *ao-shingou* (literally, blue traffic light) than *midori-ringo* (green apple) or *midori-shingou* (green traffic light) followed by the vowel "*i.*" This is because words that are easier to pronounce tend to be used more often. I have also noticed that it becomes more difficult to pronounce *midori* (green) when combined with words other than *ao*, which could explain why blue and green are still used together in the same grouping.

A more extreme example of labor reduction that appears in the Japanese classics is *saitazumairo*, a dark green color that derived from the leaves of the *itadori* (tiger grass). In the Heian period (794–1185), when the *Goshūi Wakashū* (Later Collection of Gleanings of Japanese Poems) was compiled, *saitazumairo* was the color name for everyday use.[46] Because it is difficult to read and has an extremely long pronunciation, people today rarely say, "The grass is always more *saitazumairo* on the other side." Color words that are difficult to pronounce, such as *saitazumairo*, tend to fall into disuse.

Color names can sometimes become obsolete when the source of their origin becomes extinct. For instance, the Japanese crested ibis (*toki*), which was once a common bird throughout Japan, had feathers that were used for crafts and arrow feathers. However, due to overhunting, the Japanese crested ibis became extinct in 2003, and the color name *toki-iro* (crested ibis) has now become less familiar. In contrast, flamingos are still abundant in zoos, and the color name "flamingo pink" is still used in Japan today.

There are various names for the hue of red in Japanese, namely, *beni, shu, hi, akane, suou, tan, akane, bengara, enji, taisha,* and *ko*.[47] These color names are mainly derived from dyes and pigments. One thing I

---

[46] Fujiwara no Yoshitaka (954–974), *Goshūi Wakashū* (1086), Vol. 2, Spring 149.

[47] Kunimoto, N. (2009). *The color red in 8th century Japan*, p. 252.

found strange when I translated *Basic Color Terms* was that *aka* (red) was used in Japanese as the red BCT, but in Chinese (Mandarin), it was listed as *húng* (*hung* in Cantonese).[48] Although Japanese and Chinese use the same *kanji*, aka in Japanese, *beni(húng)* in Chinese seems to have prevailed as the BCT. Why this use of different *kanji* occurred remains unknown. In Japan and Taiwanese Chinese, *aka* and *beni*, both meaning red, are often confused with each other. A perfect example of this confusion can be seen on the annual NHK (Japan Broadcasting Corporation) New Year's Eve television program *Kōhaku Uta Gassen*. The program refers to the "red group," pronounced *akagumi*, but in the notation, it is given as *benigumi*. *Aka* is an ancient Japanese color word based on the pronunciation of the expression *akarui* (bright). *Aka* has a broader meaning than *beni*. In Chinese, red symbolizes more than color; it symbolizes the communist revolution, loyalty, and exposure.[49] The Japanese word "red" also refers to a baby. By contrast, in Chinese, *húng* refers to the name of paint[50] and has a narrower range of meanings than red. As with *aka* and *beni*, the use of color names varies between dominant and subordinate.

Color names not only increase but frequently decrease, and it is not necessarily because they are traditional color names that they continue to be used.[51] Despite Japan's many traditional color names, they are not often used in everyday conversation. Nonetheless, traditional Japanese colors are a standard design element for sundries and tourist souvenirs that claim to be Japanese in style. Color charts[52] were initially marketed,

[48] *Basic Color Terms*, Japanese translation (2016), pp. 134, 153, 147.

[49] Hakusuisha, "Chinese Dictionary" https://cjjc.weblio.jp/content/赤 (Accessed: Feb 20, 2021).

[50] Hakusuisha, "Chinese Dictionary" https://cjjc.weblio.jp/content/%E7%B4%85 (Accessed: Feb 20, 2021).

[51] There are certain color names that are traditional and not commonly used in everyday speech. However, at special events such as the Emperor's coronation ceremony, ancient traditional colors may be introduced. *Korozen no goho* is an example of such a color.

[52] DIC Color Guide, *Traditional Colors of Japan* (1st ed released in 1978, 9th ed as of 2021).

and gel ink ballpoint pens,[53] a series of paints,[54] stamps, automobiles,[55] and other products with traditional color themes. A growing preference for traditional Japanese style is driving the trend. *Traditional Colors of the World* books and color charts influence design students. However, whether Japanese people come into contact with and use the various traditional color names in their daily lives in conversation and writing is another matter.

What is the "traditional color" category? Traditional colors are a category of colors that evoke "Japaneseness." Moreover, traditional colors are the names of pigments used in Japanese painting, seasonal color schemes described in the literature, and color names used in textile dyeing. Wikipedia defines the traditional colors of Japan as follows: "Traditional colors of Japan is a collection of colors traditionally used in Japanese art, literature, kimono and other textiles, and other Japanese crafts."[56]

Nagasaki, who taught at Kyoto City University of Arts, researched approximately 200 traditional Japanese color names and compiled a chronology of the periods in which they appeared in literature.[57] According to the chronology, in some periods, many color names were created (Asuka, Nara, Heian, Muromachi, Edo, and Meiji periods). The Kamakura and Sengoku periods were times of frequent outbreaks of civil wars, but unlike other periods, only a limited number of color names appeared in these periods. The increase in the number of color names was due to the implementation of sumptuary laws (see further in Chapter 7). These laws led to variations in shades of colors like indigo, which were particularly popular during the Edo period. The number of foreign loan color names has increased in the twenty-first century. The number of colors in the rainbow varies by language, and sometimes, the seven colors are reduced to six, as in the recent English language. Determining the

[53] PENTEL "Silk Story" (released in 1999).

[54] Turner Colors Corporation "Acrylic Gouache Japanesque Color," "12 Colors Set – Traditional Japanese Colors".

[55] Toyota Motor Corporation, Crown "Japan Color Selection Package (12 colors)" (2015).

[56] https://en.wikipedia.org/wiki/traditional_colors_of_japan (Accessed: Feb 21, 2021).

[57] Nagasaki, S. (1996). *Traditional Colors of Japan: Their Color Names and Color Tones* (Kyoto Shoin Arts Collection 5).

advancement of a language and culture only by looking at the number of its color names is questionable, as this number can vary.

3.7 EVOLUTION AND EUGENICS

Explaining the color vision of other races and how they name colors, without scientific evidence or in-person research, has long been a common practice in academia.[58] To disprove the prejudiced and extreme linguistic relativism[59] which claims that "people who use languages with a small vocabulary of color names do not perceive color properly," Berlin and Kay's theory suggests that there exist specific color categories that are universally present and recognized by all humans, regardless of their cultural or linguistic background.

However, as the title, *Basic Color Terms: Their Universality and Evolution*, suggests, Berlin and Kay were at least influenced by the social Darwinist and eugenic views that were common in anthropology and linguistics in the 1960s. In *Basic Color Terms*, Berlin and Kay euphemistically suggested that regions that have more BCTs are complex societies, and the regions with fewer BCTs are mostly in the tropics.

I consider in this chapter the perspective that more BCTs equates to developed complex societies.[60] In *Basic Color Terms*, Van Wijk's research compares the "hue-centric" view in languages from higher-latitude regions to the "brightness-centric" view of color in languages spoken near the Equator. He also cites a 1962 study by Richard H. Post, a eugenicist at the University of Michigan Medical School. He found that people in language groups who live "close to nature" have fewer BCTs because they have more objects to trace colors to in their environment.[61] In his essay "The North–South Problem of Food," brain scientist Kenichiro Mogi pointed out that living environments near the Equator, such as the tropics, are filled with a variety of colorful species such as fish, butterflies, parrots, and orchids. In contrast, areas farther from the Equator, like the north (temperate and subarctic), have limited color

---

[58] Saini, A. (2020). *Superior: The Return of Race Science* (E. Togo, Trans. In Japanese).

[59] Brown, D. E. (2002). *Human Universals* (Japanese edition). p. 16.

[60] Hirasawa, Y. (1997). The Problem of Cultural Development Degree from the Viewpoint of Color. pp. 17–26.

[61] Berlin & Kay (1969). *Basic Color Terms*, pp. 149–151.

diversity in their living environments due to monoculture.[62] I mostly agree with Mogi's opinion. The lack of color in the environment is not why fewer BCTs exist. Instead, I infer that people in temperate regions with less diversity in the color of their environment mass produce and define BCTs that are forced to rely on adjectives. Possibly, they are forced to increase the number of BCTs because of the lack of metaphorical objects in their living environment. A reason may be that people living in colorful environments have a greater abundance of things that can be metaphorized by the colors of their environment than those not living in colorful environments: thus, using BCTs to describe them, as in English and Japanese, is unnecessary.

One of the appendices in *Basic Color Terms* is entitled "The Growth of Color Vocabulary: One Hundred Years of Theory." In this appendix, Berlin and Kay examined the linguistics and anthropology of color and explored how linguistic relativism came to be. Scholars and missionaries from the West often traveled to yet-to-be-civilized lands or read ancient literature and encountered different color views and expressions. They then concluded that these views differed fundamentally from biological cognition because the language and logic of these cultures were different from those of Western society.

An example of the research presented in "The Growth of Color Vocabulary: One Hundred Years of Theory" is as follows. In March 1858, 111 years before the publication of *Basic Color Terms*, British Prime Minister and historian Gladstone (1809–1898) wrote the final chapter of his major work, *Studies on Homer and the Homeric Age*. Gladstone acknowledged that the Greeks of Homer's time could perceive differences in brightness or light and dark.[63] However, Gladstone, who read Homer's document literally, wrote that the ancient Greeks were less developed or more color-blind than modern humans. He based this notion of underdevelopment or colorblindness on Homer's description of the "wine-dark sea,"[64] and Homer's use of the word *glauk'os* for willow, olive, and papyrus leaves, despite it usually referring to eye color. The word *glauk'os* originally meant "glowing or shining" without reference to color, and this word has

---

[62] Mogi, K. (2006). The North-South Problem of Food. *Qualia of Food*, pp. 168–176.

[63] Berlin & Kay (1969). *Basic Color Terms*, pp. 134–135.

[64] *Oinops póntos* (οἶνοψ πόντος). John Mackey's *Wine-Dark Sea*, a piece for brass band, quotes Homer's expression in its title.

3 CATEGORIZING COLORS BY NAME   67

further come to mean "silvery-white" as well. Gladstone's logic assumes Prince was colorblind because he sang *Purple Rain*, but it may be a poetic metaphor by Homer.

Since the time of the ancient Greeks, when Theophrastos (371–287 BCE), a naturalist of the Aristotelian school, wrote *Flora* (c. 314 BCE), Europe has had a long history of botany. Observing and recording plants was conducted by classifying plant varieties by form, color, and other characteristics and grouping similar plants into species. In Europe and the Middle East, royalty and aristocrats collected specimens of rare plants, animals, and minerals as a hobby.

After the Age of Discovery, when France and England expanded their colonies far from their home countries, explorers and scholars found many plants, animals, and ores that did not exist in Europe. Furthermore, from the late nineteenth century onward, the evolutionary theories of Charles Robert Darwin (1809–1882) and Ernst Heinrich Philipp August Haeckel (1834–1919), phylogenetic taxonomy, the collection, classification, systematization, and conservation of plants and animals in evolutionary phylogeny, became mainstream among biologists. When Darwin set out on his research voyage aboard the *Beagle*, he carried a book of color charts called *Werner's Nomenclature of Colours*.[65] Color charts were an essential tool for observing plants, animals, and ores and for establishing standard colors, and the demand for them was increasing. Systematic taxonomy flourished, especially in England, as scholars sought to test the Darwinian evolutionary theory on newly discovered organisms in Australia, New Zealand, Africa, and Latin America. Evolutionists called evolution the change from simple to complex.

Until the mid-twentieth century, an extreme linguistic relativism[66] was prevalent, such that people who used languages with small color-word vocabularies might not perceive color correctly. People whose color-word concepts, divisions, and number of color words differed from those of Europeans were regarded as less evolved than the latter. However, in 1957, 12 years before the publication of Berlin and Kay's study, the concept of "universal grammar," a turning point in the universality of human language, was introduced by Noam Chomsky, a cognitive

[65] Syme, P. (1821). *Werner's Nomenclature of Colours, with additions arranged to render it highly useful to the arts and sciences. Annexed to which are examples selected from well-known objects in the animal, vegetable, and mineral kingdoms.*

[66] Brown. (1991). *Human Universals*. McGraw-Hill Humanities Social.

68   K. HIDAKA

science linguist and philosopher at Massachusetts Institute of Technology, who published it in his book, *Syntactic Structures*. The theory is that humans are born with the basic ability to understand and speak a language and that all languages have a generally fixed pattern. I fully agree with Chomsky's theory that most humans have eyes, mouths, ears, and universal physical language abilities. However, I doubt the extent of universality and commonality in grammar and vocabulary. The number of languages is estimated to be close to 20,000, and there are probably language concepts that do not fit the definition of Berlin and Kay's colorful language evolution model.

The late 1960s, when *Basic Color Terms* was published, roughly coincided with the period immediately after the passage of the US Civil Rights Act of 1964. At this time, the deprivation of voting rights for people of color, the elimination of racial segregation in schools and public facilities, and racial discrimination were discussed. Against this backdrop, there was a major shift from the era when the belief was that people of different races and languages had fundamentally different worldviews, and the theory of linguistic universality, which asserts that people see color and other things in the same way, spread rapidly.

Color names increase and decrease worldwide for various reasons, such as dividing colors into small parts, grouping colors into large parts, or starting to use foreign words. These differences have created diversity. However, the level of cultural development and evolution of other languages and cultures is based on something other than the viewpoint and criteria that languages and cultures differ.

3.8   Do Basic Color Terms (BCTs) and Traditional Color Names Matter for Gender?

I found the color chart in Fig. 3.5 on the Internet.[67] The author of the color chart, widely circulated on social networking sites around 2010, is unknown. The man on the right categorizes colors into seven names, while the woman on the left divides them into 29. The right side is primarily BCTs, while the left is all conventional color names. This color chart hints at the stereotype that men represent colors in the

---

[67] http://linguisticanthropology.org/blog/2010/03/11/basic-color-terms-gender-stereotypes/ (Accessed: Feb 24, 2021).

broad BCT category while women represent colors in the more detailed and emotive idiomatic color names. The Society for Linguistic Anthropology's website introduces the chart in Fig. 3.5 as an excellent graphic example that simultaneously illustrates Deborah Cameron's study of intergender communication and Berlin and Kay's BCTs, since the relationship between BCTs and gender stereotypes is prominently represented in this chart.

There are likely differences between men and women in the way they see and categorize colors and in the way they name colors. This is because the incidence of color weakness and color blindness is genetically much higher in males than in females (the incidence also varies across races). Color weakness/blindness is a condition in which one of the three components of color vision—red, green, and blue—is challenging to see, or color is unrecognizable due to the functional characteristics of the retina cones. Although this can be acquired, many cases are congenital and genetic. In the case of the Japanese, 5% of males are born with a color

Fig. 3.5 Color categorization and gender stereotype

weakness or color blindness, while only 0.2% of females are. Females have two X chromosomes; therefore, the mutation will not be expressed if one chromosome is mutated. Males, however, have only one X chromosome; therefore, a mutation in one of the chromosomes increases the probability of expression. This is acknowledged to be the reason why the probability of color blindness is higher in males.[68]

The difference in the response of men and women to color brought about by genetic factors has also been indicated by primate research. Primatologist Toshisada Nishida has theorized that the reason men were more likely to be hunters and women plant gatherers is that women are better judges of color and, thus, are less likely to choose immature or poisonous foods, such as poisonous mushrooms; this is considered a leading theory.[69] According to Nishida, biological inheritance and cultural practices make women more capable of distinguishing colors in detail, especially those related to plant gathering and cooking. This also explains why women are more interested in color from a clothing and cosmetics marketing perspective. As a result, clothing stores tend to offer a wider range of color options for women than for men.

However, being a woman does not mean being particular about everything. In a figure posted on the Internet at one point that refuted the notion that women are more meticulous about color than men are about other things, trains, machines, and automobiles were cited as examples of objects that men classify more finely. There are certainly many women who are not interested in color, and there are certainly men who classify the colors of objects in which they are interested in more detail, so categorizing by gender alone is not a simple explanation. The level of detail in color categorization varies from subject to subject and individual to individual.

[68] https://www.cbsnews.com/news/race-gender-color-blindness-risk/ (Accessed: Feb 24, 2021).

[69] Nishida, T. (2007). *Where Did Humanity Come from: An Approach from Primate Studies.*

CHAPTER 4

Categorizing Colors by Criteria

All colors are the friends of their neighbors and the lovers of their opposites.
Marc Chagall

Marc Chagall (1887–1986), a Jewish painter from Belarus, used relations of colors on a color wheel to describe human relationships. He likened similar colors next to each other on the circumference of the color wheel (red and orange, or yellow-green and green, etc.) to friends, and colors on opposite sides of the color wheel (red versus green, yellow versus purple, etc.) to lovers because of the strong contrast between them. Chagall's paintings seem to have been created from his knowledge of color theory and his warm and humanistic handling of color.

This chapter will demonstrate how to categorize colors by criteria or standards. The problem with using only color names to represent colors is that it creates color categories with relatively many color names in common with humanity and categories with few color names. Colors in the hard-to-name category range cannot be communicated, and color names cannot accurately represent all colors. The same phenomenon occurred during the Berlin and Kay survey, with approximately 70% of the

© The Author(s), under exclusive license to Springer Nature
Switzerland AG 2024
K. Hidaka, *The Art of Color Categorization*,
https://doi.org/10.1007/978-3-031-47690-7_4

survey color chart being in the unnamed zone.[1] It is impossible to accurately convey subtle color differences to others using only color names. Color categories that cannot be fully expressed by color names exist across the color chart like unexplored, uncharted territory. To gather all these categories and communicate them to others, researchers have sought an ideal standard for classifying colors. This chapter introduces some of these attempts at categorization standards and methods of expression, such as determining basic colors, assigning degrees of purity and rank order, applying them to figures, assigning attributes, and quantifying them. Just as the number of colors in a rainbow differs by country and language, there are numerous criteria and methods for sorting colors.

4.1 Primary Colors

A color that can be mixed to create other colors is called a primary color in color science terminology. A primary color is a color that cannot be created by mixing other colors. Scholars in different countries have various theories about primary colors. Every year I ask my college classes: "What is the minimum number of colors you need for yourself to mix colors to create a color painting?" The answers vary from around five colors to 20. However, most people answer that the minimum five colors are red, blue, yellow, green, and black; thus, it can be assumed that the primary or essential colors exist for humans. It is similar to cooking, where some people cook with only salt, pepper, and sugar, whereas others need soy sauce, miso, mirin (sweet sake), dashi stock, various oils and liquors, and various spices and herbs.

> *Although we have only five colors, we can create a wide variation of colors by combining those five colors and achieve victory.*
> Sun Tzu, *The Art of War*, Vol. 5.

In *the Art of War*, written during the Spring and Autumn and Warring States Period (515–350 BCE) in China, Sun Tzu observes that although there are only five colors (red, blue, yellow, white, and black) that are the elements of various colors, a variety of colors can be created by mixing these colors. Given the lack of green in the five Chinese primary colors,

---

[1] Berlin, B., & Kay, P. (1969). *Basic Color Terms: Their Universality and Evolution*, p. 10.

I can assume that in China, either blue or black also meant green. The definition of "primary color" is currently imprecise,[2] and in Japan, many people even consider primary color to mean a flashy, vivid color.

Although there are several typical theories on the number of primary colors, the basis for determining them differs, and there is no correct answer.

4.1.1 Red, Yellow, Blue, White, Black (R, Y, B, W, K) Theory

Symbols for taste, internal organs, direction, seasons, imaginary animals = primary colors.

The oldest traditional primary colors are the five Chinese colors: red, yellow, blue, white, and black. These five colors belong to the five elements philosophy (the theory that all things are composed of the five elements: fire, water, wood, metal, and earth), and the source is said to be the *Inner Canon of the Yellow Emperor*[3] (circa 475–221 BCE), which is the oldest work on Chinese medicine and has been selected for UNESCO's Memory of the World Program. These five colors classify tastes, organs, directions, seasons, and mythological creatures.

> Red: bitter = heart, small intestine = fire = summer = South = Vermilion bird
> Yellow: sweet = stomach = soil = center = earth
> Blue: acid = liver, gall = wood = East = spring = Blue dragon
> White: spicy = lungs, large intestine = gold = autumn = West = White tiger
> Black: salty = kidney = water = winter = North = Black tortoise

The color categorization of these symbols retains vestiges of Asian cultures influenced by China and India. The Chinese five colors have long influenced all areas of life even though they have no scientific basis. In the twentieth century, the five colors were also used as a symbol of the "Republic of the Five Tribes," a political slogan of the government of the Republic of China in Beijing, aiming at cooperation among the Han,

---

[2] Kuehni, R. G., & Schwartz, A. (2008). *Color Ordered: A Survey of Color Systems from Antiquity to the Present*. Oxford University Press, p. 380.

[3] In the Basic Questions of *the Inner Canon of the Yellow Emperor*.

74   K. HIDAKA

Manchu, Mongolian, Uyghur, and Tibetan ethnic groups; however, there is no specific color distinction as to which color is for which ethnic group.

4.1.2   *Red, Yellow, Black, Blue (R, Y, K, B) Theory/White, Yellow, Red, Black (W, Y, R, K) Theory*

Red, yellow, black, blue (R, Y, K, B) theory: colors of human temperament = primary colors
or
White, yellow, red, black (W, Y, R, K) theory: base colors to be mixed in paint = primary colors.

Ancient Greece also categorized colors, but there are two types here: human bodily fluids and the primary colors of paint. Both primary color categories have four colors.

The first is the primary color, which Hippocrates of Kos (c. 460–370 BCE), a physician who influenced European and Arabic-Indian medicine, applied to the four temperaments based on the four humors. He suggested that the following basic dispositions existed.

> Red: sanguine, cheerful, and vivacious = air
> Yellow: choleric, short-tempered and excitable = fire
> Black: melancholic, careful = ground
> Blue: phlegmatic, sympathetic = water

The application of color to temperament became commonplace. In Aristotle's (384–322 BCE) essay *On Colors*,[4] dated around 300 BCE, he wrote that colors follow the four elements (air, fire, earth, and water) related to the four temperaments, which influenced the standards for color categorization in later European culture.

The second primary color is the primary color for painting. In the encyclopedia *Natural History* by Pliny the Great (Plinius Maior, or Gaius Plinius Secundus, 23–79 CE), a Greek painter named Apelles of Kos, who lived around the fourth century BCE, appears. Although no works by

---

[4] It is attributed to Aristotle, but the translator's commentary mentions the possibility of a treatise by the Aristotelian school. *The Complete Works of Aristotle* 10, (1969), p. 324.

Apelles have survived, the four-color palette (*tetrachromatikón*[5]), namely, white, yellow, red, and black, is known as the primary colors of ancient Greek art. The raw materials are the white of plaster, the yellow of yellow ochre, the red of sinopia, and the black of oily smoke or charcoal.

These two types, body fluids and paint, have long been dominant in European science and art.

4.1.3   Red, Yellow, Blue (R, Y, B) Theory

Base colors to be mixed in paint = primary colors.

The three primary color theory (1831), where red, yellow, and blue are the basic colors of paints to be mixed for painting, was proposed by Sir David Brewster (1781–1868), a British scientist and inventor. The colors produced by mixing the primary colors of red, yellow, and blue (such as orange from mixing red and yellow, green from mixing yellow and blue, and purple from mixing red and blue) are called secondary colors. Colors created by mixing secondary colors are called tertiary colors. White is omitted because there is no paint, and black is the color created by mixing everything.

4.1.4   Red, Green, Blue (R, G, B) Theory

Color of light based on visual cells = primary colors.

The Young–Helmholtz theory of the three primary colors (1850) claims red, green, and blue, to which the cone cells in the human retina respond. The German physiologist and physicist Hermann Ludwig Ferdinand von Helmholtz (1821–1894) proposed the theory by the English physicist Thomas Young (1773–1829). Many people have heard that the three primary colors of light are RGB (red, green, and blue) and the four primary colors of colorants are CMYK (cyan, magenta, yellow, and black). The colors displayed on computers, LCD TV screens, and projectors use these RGB light colors to display images. The lighter, the brighter (more energy is added). Hence, the term "additive color mixing" is used for this mixing.

---

[5] https://www.massey.ac.nz/massey/learning/departments/school-of-humanities/classical-world-new-zealand/visual-arts/raemon-rolfe.cfm (Accessed: Feb. 25, 2021).

76   K. HIDAKA

4.1.5   Red ↔ Green, Yellow ↔ Blue, White ↔ Black (R ↔ G, Y ↔ B, W ↔ B) Theory

Psychological color based on afterimage = primary color.

The German physiologist Karl Ewald Konstantin Hering (1834–1918) proposed complementary colors, or the opponent process, to explain the afterimage of the eye, where white ↔ black, red ↔ green, yellow ↔blue are the primary colors. It is also called the theory of the four primary colors of psychology (1878). The psychological primary colors incorporate colors seen as afterimages and are based on six colors: four colors (red, green, yellow, and blue) plus two colors (white and black).

Complementary color afterimages occur in the human eye. This is a phenomenon in which a color is visible even when it disappears from view after one has been gazing at it for a while. For example, if you have been staring at red for a long time, it is easy to see the complementary color blue-green (cyan). Red, yellow, and white cause the breakdown (or catabolic process) of their respective receptors, the retinal cells, whereas green, blue, and black cause their respective receptors' accumulation (or anabolic process). At the height of the Renaissance, 300 years before Hering's time, the scientist and artist Leonardo Da Vinci (1452–1519) wrote in his *Treatise on Painting* that "white, yellow, green, blue, red, and black are the six single colors, white and black, red and green, and yellow and blue complement each other."[6] Da Vinci recorded the contrasting relationships of the four primary colors in an age when even the concept of complementary colors was unknown. These four primary psychological colors are also related to the concepts explained in Chapter 3 (see Sect. 3.2).

4.1.6   Red, Yellow, Green, Blue, Purple (R, Y, G, B, P) Theory

Colors that become gray by rotational mixing = primary colors.

Rotational color mixing is an experimental technique, where an object painted with multiple colors is rotated to obtain mixed colors. In his *Opticks* (1704), Newton demonstrated that white is made up of many colors because when the colors of the rainbow are made into rings and rotated at high speed, they appear white due to afterimages. In physics,

---

[6] Da Vinci, L. (1892). *Treatise on Painting*. Rigaud, J., and Brown, W. B. A. (Trans.), p. 99.

this colored disk is called Newton's disk, and scientists since Newton have used a rotating color-mixing machine and disk in experiments to mix the colors of light. This has become an essential experimental apparatus for the study of color.

Art educator and painter Munsell's theory of the five primary colors (1905) includes red, yellow, green, blue, and purple. These are the primary colors for rotational color mixing. Munsell developed the color chart used in Berlin and Kay's research. The Munsell color system evolved into the JIS (Japanese Industrial Standards). Munsell's method of determining primary colors is based on the fact that when colors on opposite sides of a color wheel are rotated and mixed, they become gray. There is no answer to the question as to why gray was chosen as the standard. It is conceivable that gray has been influenced by the history of the importance placed on drawing, which depicts grayscale tones in Western painting, and by the traditional emphasis on gray.[7]

In 1900, Munsell patented the color sphere. The color sphere was a physical three-dimensional representation of colors in a sphere to display the three parameters of the three attributes. These five primary colors were the colors that appeared gray when this globe-like color sphere was rotated and mixed. Munsell thought Brewster's three primary colors and Hering's four primary colors were wrong because they did not produce gray even when rotated and mixed. Furthermore, Munsell was particular about the numbers five and ten, using the finger-countable decimal system for his color system and specifying a median value of 5.0R and N5.0. The combinations red and blue-green, yellow and blue-violet, green and red-violet, blue and yellow–red, and purple and yellow-green produce gray with relatively little coloration. However, because of the low demand for gray that should be mixed, Munsell's five primary colors were not extensively used as the elemental primary colors for color mixing.

4.1.7 Cyan, Magenta, Yellow, and Black (C, M, Y, K)

Color for printing = primary color.

In 1906, the Eagle Printing Ink Company first adopted four-color process inks for wet printing: cyan, magenta, yellow, and black. The four primary colors of CMYK are the colors of books, magazines, photographs,

---

[7] In the film *Fifty Shades of Gray,* the idiomatic phrase "shades of gray" and the fact that the name of the protagonist is Gray is used as a hook.

and photocopier and printer toners printed on paper. These four CMYK colors could be combined to produce a wide range of rich color numbers, and they became the standard primary colors in the printing industry. The color CMYK is a decomposition of RGB (additive mixed color). For example, to produce red R in printing, magenta and yellow are layered on top of each other, cyan and yellow are layered to produce green G, and cyan and magenta are layered to produce blue B.

4.2 Pure Colors

Pure color (*Vollfarben* in German, full color, literally in English) is subtly similar to but distinct from primary colors. Pure colors are based on Hering's four primary colors: red, green, yellow, and blue. Friedrich Wilhelm Ostwald (1853–1932), a Latvian-born Nobel laureate in chemistry, proposed the concept of "pure color," free of black, white, and impurities. He divided colors into a hierarchy of three groups.

First group (neutral color): only black and white colors.
Second group (full color): pure colors that do not include black or white. Ultramarine blue is placed as the diagonal of yellow and sea green as the opposite of red.
Third group (dull color, or veiled colors): pure colors mixed with black or white.

According to Ostwald, any color can be represented by rotational mixing based on these three variables of ideal black (B), ideal white (W), and ideal pure color (F) in their respective area ratios. The theory is that all colors are made of white quantity (W) + black quantity (B) + pure color (F) = 100% and can be obtained from rotational mixing.[8]

Another concept of color perception similar to pure color is unique hue, which describes a color that, like a pure color, is perceived as if it is not mixed with any other color.[9] Red, yellow, green, and blue are unique hues, but experiments show that people differ in what they consider unique hues.

[8] https://www.colorsystem.com/?page_id=862&lang=en (Accessed: Feb. 24, 2021).

[9] Miyahara, E. (2003). *Focal Colors and Unique Hues*, pp. 1038–1042.

4 CATEGORIZING COLORS BY CRITERIA   79

The Munsell color chart used by Berlin and Kay in their experiments presented the concept of a focal color. A focal color is one that stands out (salient) on a color chart and typically appears to be the color of that name, while a pure color is a color that is psychologically perceived as pure. Notably, colors selected for a focal color are similar to those selected for a pure color or unique hue.

It is important to note the distinction between pure colors and mixed colors. Ostwald's notion of colors that appear pure and unmixed is difficult to define both psychologically and physically. It appears to have been common to science in the first half of the twentieth century. The idea of pure-bred animals, as opposed to hybrids, was popular in Europe from the 19th to the twentieth century. For example, when animal breeders avoid crossbreeding to maintain pedigree purebreds, it reflects the idea of avoidance of mixing. The Ostwaldian concept of color categorization, "pure color plus white or black," was carried over in the Natural Color System (NCS), a Swedish industrial standard, and is still used today. This color categorization reflects biology's idea of the distinction between "pure" and "mixed" colors.

4.3   RANKING

There is no autonomous ranking of naturally occurring colors. However, humans have classified colors according to their order and assigned them a rank and pecking order.

According to Goethe in his *Theory of Colors* (*Zur Farbenlehre*, 1810), the first color is white.[10] Following white, says Goethe, all colors are synthesized from red and black. The basis for the order of colors is the order in which sulfur burns. When sulfur burns, pale green and yellow appear first, followed by scarlet and blue. Goethe's correlation between the order of colors and the burning of sulfur is similar to that of color temperature. The unit of color temperature is Kelvin (K), which is a measure of the color of illumination when shooting with a camera. It is proportional to the color of an object when it burns, with blue and white having higher color temperatures and yellow and red having lower color temperatures. In other words, a hot gas burner produces a blue flame, whereas a candle or a match burns at a lower temperature and

---

[10] Goethe, J. W. von. (1999). *Theory of Colors*, Vol. 2 (History), pp. 245–247.

80   K. HIDAKA

appears orange. Thus, on the scale of color temperature, blue and white are considered high-color temperature colors, whereas yellow, orange, and red are low-color temperature colors.

Furthermore, Goethe uses the term *Steigerung* (high ascent or increase) to refer to a decrease of the dimness of color as a change in color.[11] This term seems to refer to a state in which colors change more vividly and is found in some Goethe-inspired treatises on art, literary history, and other subjects. Goethe called significant shifts in hue, such as yellow turning to ruby, *Steigerung*, a term questionable in color science. These ideas of color ranking were popularized through translations of *Theory of Colors* into various European languages.

The concept of color ranking also exists in Brewster's theory of red, yellow, and blue (R, Y, B)—the base colors to be mixed in paint (see Sect. 4.1.3). The word primary means "first." This red, yellow, and blue theory has the concept of the order of primary, secondary, and tertiary colors. In the case of paint, white is the highest-ranking color, and the more colors are mixed, the lower the ranking becomes, approaching black, the lowest-ranking color. Adding the primary colors red and yellow produces orange. Similarly, adding yellow and blue produces green, and adding red and blue produces purple. Colors such as orange, green, and purple are called secondary colors when mixed. Next, color variations mixed with secondary colors are called tertiary colors (e.g., vermilion, amber, chartreuse, teal,[12] violet, and magenta).

The writings of scholars such as Goethe and Brewster had a significant impact on the ranking of colors. Many European researchers began to rank the colors of nature from the human point of view, no ranking having previously existed.

[11] Goethe, (translated into Japanese, 1999). *Theory of Colors*, Vol. 1 (Chapter 38, "517 The High Ascent of Color" p. 204).

[12] Chartreuse is a color between yellow and green derived from a liqueur produced in 1764 at the Cartesian monastery of Grande Chartreuse in France. Making this liqueur is still considered a secret known only to three monks. Teal is the color of a duck's feathers and the blue-green color of a mallard's head.

4.4 ATTRIBUTES

How can we accurately describe the colors we see other than by using color names? In the early twentieth century the United States was the first country to notate color quantitatively, making widespread use of the three attributes of color: hue, brightness (lightness), and saturation (vividness).

Munsell created the three-attribute color scale and was the founder of the Munsell Color Company and the publisher of the Munsell color chart. His Munsell color system is a combination of hue (the colors of the rainbow, i.e., red = R, green = G, etc.), value (lightness of color, expressed in ten steps), and chroma (saturation of color) of each hue, expressed in the order hue value/chroma. For example, "2R 6/8" means that 2R is red, 6/8 is lightness 6, and saturation 8. The Munsell color system is one of the most concise color systems to define the concept of the three attributes.

Let us now review the definition of the color communication system and what properties it possesses. Nemcsics, a Hungarian color designer and university faculty member, working with colleagues, described the following:

a. A system for classifying colors. Colors are arranged according to some rules by human color perception, color stimulus, or object color.
b. A set of colors by the three attributes that make up the coordinates in the color space.
c. A reasonable graphic to indicate and identify the color of an object using a standard color chart.[13]

The Munsell Color Company, which Munsell founded until its closure in the 1970s, sold the Munsell color chart and other color charts for photography, soil, and food. Munsell is thought to have proposed the idea of quantitative notation when teaching painting to his students, as he wanted to indicate colors rather than using color names.

Munsell's book, *A Color Notation* (1905), explains the concept of the color system and its three attributes. At the beginning of the book, Munsell described the difficulty and necessity of communicating

---

[13] Caivano, J. L., & Nemcsics, A. (2022). Color Order Systems, p. 1.

82   K. HIDAKA

color names by quoting a letter from the Scottish writer Robert Louis Stevenson (1850–1894), who wrote *Dr Jekyll and Mr Hyde* and *Treasure Island*:

> *Well, I'll be hanged if I can describe this red—it's not Turkish and it's not Roman and it's not Indian, but it seems to partake of the two last, and yet it can't be either of them because it ought to be able to go with vermilion. Ah, what a tangled web we weave—anyway, with what brains you have left choose me and send some–many—patterns of this exact shade.*[14]

In this letter Stevenson, who had moved to Upolu, Samoa,[15] is requesting wallpaper samples from his friend Colvin in London. Stevenson attempts to describe the red color on the walls of his small workroom in as many cultural descriptions (Turkish, Roman, Indian) as he can. Instead of describing it with these cultural adjectives, Stevenson could have written "light," "dark," or "bright," and he would not have been buried in a pile of "some–many—patterns of this exact shade" wallpaper. In quoting this sentence, Munsell was attempting to show that even if a well-known writer uses all the color names and adjectives he can find, he will never be able to convey color names exactly. Various color names have an imaginative and poetic quality. However, like the wallpaper in Stevenson's room, they cannot be a precise means of communicating color in industry and design.[16]

Thus, the systematization and quantitative notation of colors began in industry when people started to realize the contradictions and limitations[17] of communicating colors by color name alone. Munsell expressed his reason for developing color standards such as the color system in the twentieth century thus: "It would, of course, be a waste of time to attempt the naming of every kind and degree of color."[18]

---

[14] Stevenson, R. L. (1901). *Vailima Letters* (p. 194). Scribner's Bookstore.
Munsell, A. H. (1967). *A Color Notation* (12th edition). Munsell Color Company, p. 13.

[15] Samoa is now a member of the British Commonwealth, but in the nineteenth century, it was a territory of the United States and Germany.

[16] Munsell, A. H. (2009). *A Color Notation* (Hidaka, Trans.). "Translator's Afterword," p. 71.

[17] Omi, G. (1983). *A History of Color and World Affairs*, pp. 32–33.

[18] Munsell, A. H. (1967). *A Color Notation* (12th edition). Munsell Color Company, p. 14.

4 CATEGORIZING COLORS BY CRITERIA   83

It is surprising that before the end of the nineteenth century, there was no quantitative standard for color notation. The Industrial Revolution in England in the eighteenth century brought about mass production through industrialization. It also began the compression and rationalization of labor and material costs in industrial production. Colonial policy was advanced as labor and materials were actively procured overseas due to territorial expansion in the name of imperialism. At any rate, the expansion of colonization and industrialization made it an urgent task to accurately convey colors to foreigners with different languages.

Munsell was not the first to create the concept of a three-attribute color notation that accurately conveys colors. Two important figures influenced Munsell's invention of the color system.

The first was James Clerk Maxwell (1831–1879), a 19th-century English physicist, who defined the proposed color categories as "tint," "shade," and "hue." A tint is a color made by adding white to a pure color, whereas a shade is a color made by adding black to a pure color. It is close to the idea of the Ostwald color system of the twentieth century (see Sect. 4.2).[19] Maxwell's rotational color mixing, where complementary (opposite) colors are rotated at high speed to create gray, was applied to Munsell's color system.

The second was the 19th-century American physicist Ogden Nicholas Rood (1841–1902), whose book *Modern Chromatics* (1879) inspired the creation of Munsell's color system. Rood proposed the color wheel and three attributes: hue, purity, and luminosity.

Munsell's three attributes and color order system are a good combination of Maxwell's rotational color mixing and Rood's three attributes, simplified and described by symbols. The attributes and system were more precise than color names and provided an easy-to-understand standard for accurately communicating the colors, especially to factory workers in mass production.

---

[19] In the Ostwald color system, white or black is added to pure colors in a rotational mixture to determine the degree of mixing.

4.5 Color Wheels and Color Spaces

Thus far, we have looked at categorizing colors based on their attributes and standards. Next, we will introduce the concept of classifying colors by applying figures and numerical values to them. This approach uses an old analogy, a method of expression that makes information more accessible to understand by applying geometric figures based on similarity.

The idea of harmonic theory, which held that the entire universe was composed of mathematical or geometric proportions, was common in ancient Greece. In the European cultural sphere, where the influence of ancient Greece and Rome was strong, the systematic arrangement of colors on geometric figures (circles, polygons, spheres, and solids) became widespread.

A color wheel, or color circle, is an artificially created display of colors arranged in a circle, and is thought to have originated from mandalas and medieval medical diagrams. Figure 4.1 is a medieval color wheel of the color of urine. The color wheel is not only a circular arrangement of the colors of the rainbow but also explains physiological perceptual phenomena such as complementary color afterimages. In many color wheels, hue varies continuously, with hues divided by a scale or degree. When a 360-degree color wheel is used for color schemes and instructions in design and painting, it is common to divide and number the rings into 12 or 24, the common multiples of three, four, and six[20] (see Fig. 4.2, the simplified color wheel in *A Color Notation*). At first glance, it appears that there is an immutable standard for the arrangement and numbering of colors; however, unsurprisingly, it is up to the individual to decide which side of the 360-degree circumference to start numbering from.

Furthermore, the direction of rotation can be either way. The Munsell color system in the US starts from red and rotates clockwise, whereas the Ostwald color system in Germany starts from yellow and goes counterclockwise. This is a world where the first to establish and disseminate the rules wins. The same is true of automobile steering wheels, where in Japan and the United Kingdom, the steering wheel is on the right side, while in the United States and Germany it is on the left. Colorful and beautiful two-dimensional color systems have been proposed, including color wheels, triangles, squares, and stars (Fig. 4.3).

---

[20] Fukuda, K. (2012). *New Edition: Dictionary of Color Names 507*, p. 10.

4 CATEGORIZING COLORS BY CRITERIA   85

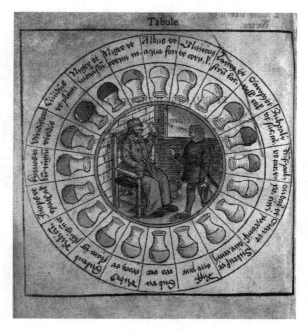

Fig. 4.1 A color wheel for urinalysis of European medical treatment (1506) (*Source* Wellcome Collection)

Colors can be indicated using three scales (hue, value, or lightness, and chroma or saturation). Because colors have vectors in these three directions, they must be three-dimensional to be visualized. The color space was created to identify colors numerically and quantitatively in three-dimensional coordinates. In the twentieth century, various forms of color space and cubes were proposed. Influenced by the color spheres painted by the German Romantic painter Philipp Otto Runge (1777–1810), Munsell wished to "create a beautiful perfect sphere of color cubes," like a globe. At first, Munsell applied the three attributes of color to a perfect sphere to visualize them in three dimensions. In doing so, he aimed for a state in which the color cubes of the Munsell color system, such as a globe, were rotated and mixed to appear gray, as an excellent color balance. For this purpose, Munsell created a color sphere that can rotate on the earth's axis, as depicted in Fig. 4.4.

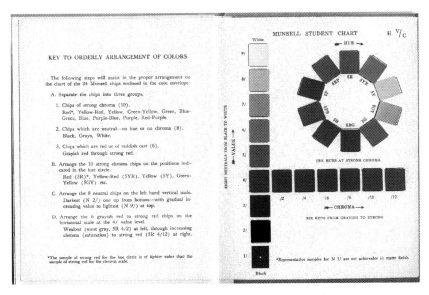

Fig. 4.2 Appendix for students of A Color Notation (1971) (*Source* Koji Ogata. *Note* Color panels on Munsell color system diagram, 10 hues on the color wheel, 9 levels of lightness, 7 levels of red saturation. In the lightness steps on the left, the white is at the top, while the black is at the bottom)

However, according to Munsell, the ideal sphere is a logical breakdown that does not actually represent reality. The Munsell color system represents the perceptual color space to the extent that it is possible to print with pigments. For this reason, even if the colors of the paint are arranged in order of vividness, they do not form a beautiful perfect sphere because different hues have different saturation levels. For example, highly saturated yellows are also high in luminosity, whereas highly saturated greens, blues, and purples are low. This alone means that the shape of Munsell's color cubes differs in terms of maximum saturation spread for each hue. Because red pigments can be more vividly colored than green, the maximum saturation of red spreads more than that of green, distorting the sphere. If more vivid pigments were invented, the Munsell

Fig. 4.3 Johannes Itten (1921) Color sphere in 7 light levels and 12 tones (Die Farbenkugel) (*Source* © VG Bild-Kunst Photo: Vitra Design Museum. *Note* 47.3 × 31.9 cm A color illustration of Bruno Adler's Utopia depicts a color sphere with white on top and black on the base)

Fig. 4.4 Color sphere of Munsell Color Company (*Source* Massachusetts College of Art and Design. *Note* When rotated, gray appears. Munsell's goal was to create a color space that resembled a globe)

color scale and color chart saturation would need to be updated. In 1856, the chemist Sir William Henry Perkin (1838–1907) invented the world's first artificial dye, a brilliant purple-mauve dye. Thanks to innovative technology, the first half of the twentieth century saw the invention of more synthetic dyes, pigments, and colorants that were even more brilliant in other hues. With these inventions, the Munsell color scale had to be revised to represent highly saturated colors.

As a compromise to solve the dilemma of different saturation levels, Munsell created the Color Tree (Fig. 4.5) analogous to the Tree of

Knowledge, which connects the heavens to the underworld, and the Tree of Life, which connects all forms of creation. Both are forms of the World Tree or Cosmic Tree, a widespread myth or archetype in various religions and philosophies. The explanation of the hue of the long branches and that of the short branches should have allowed us to follow the difference in saturation levels; however, the shape of this tree cannot be rotated to make it gray. As a result of the increasing contradiction between explanation and reality, the color sphere and the color tree originally proposed by Munsell were removed from the illustrations in the later reprint of *A Color Notation*.

Thus, the color system is a visualization of geometric figures developed in Europe by applying colors to them, and these figures are frequently shaped in such a way that white is placed high and black is placed at the bottom. Based on the principle of mixing paints and inks, the color system also created a pecking order of colors that do not exist in nature, creating the concept that unlike pure colors, as colors are mixed, they become closer to black. The color system projects this European view of the world.

How colors are divided and arranged to convey colors has developed through trial and error, and each person has their own standard for primary colors, rank, and attributes. As the number of colors in a rainbow varies, it is natural that there are various ways to divide, arrange, and communicate colors according to the time and purpose.

4.6 Color Standards and Foods

Riding the wave of the times, Munsell quickly became the man of the hour, and in 1917, a year before his death, he established a company called Munsell Color Company, which began selling standard color charts, color-measuring equipment, and color teaching materials. Originally, Munsell color charts were designed for art education, but the story of their widespread use for unanticipated purposes is not so well known. Three examples illustrate globalization and the spread of the mass production society from the United States.

After Munsell's death, the first time the Munsell color chart was selected as the color system for a national standard in the United States was in the agricultural field. It was adopted by the Agricultural Service as the standard for determining soil color, which is one of the indicators of soil composition. The United States, with its large land area and

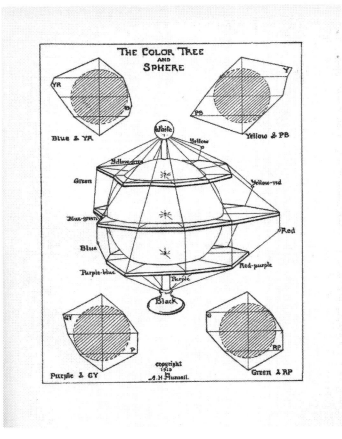

Fig. 4.5 The color tree and sphere in A Color Notation (1916) (*Note* The concept of the Munsell color tree and color space distorted by different saturation steps for each hue)

rapidly growing population, was beginning mass production of food on large farms and in factories at the beginning of the twentieth century. The Munsell Color Company also produced and sold a color chart to determine the color of frozen French fries, which was used as a standard to eliminate defective products. Even today, color measurement is critical for quality control of factory-produced food. The color of factory-produced food is judged to be within the required standards using visual inspection and color-measuring machines. In other words, the color chart is critical as a guide to determine if food is overcooked, undercooked, or discolored. There are also various color charts for judging whether a fruit is ripe. In large factories, Munsell color charts were used by employees to identify defective food products and packages.

The Munsell Color Company also created a color chart used by the Hershey Company, famous for its chocolate (Fig. 4.6). This chart was used to establish a baseline for the packaging color of the company's product, Reeses Peanut Butter Cups, so that they would not appear in different colors from different viewing angles. Reeses Peanut Butter Cups are chocolate candy with peanut butter. The combination is reminiscent of the peanut butter and jelly (the jelly is often grape-flavored) sandwich, a popular snack for American children. Thanks in part to this sandwich (abbreviated as PBS&J), the peanut butter-filled confection is a national dish for Americans. The color chart that defines the orange color used for the Reeses Peanut Butter Cups packaging became the instrument for determining the color of one of America's national dishes.

Because of the rapid increase in immigration to the United States in the first half of the twentieth century, the mass production of food in factories became a higher priority in art education than in other fields, such as color instruction. Interestingly, the Munsell color chart became more popular for determining color standards for soil, factory-produced food, and packaging than for art education, which was its original intent.

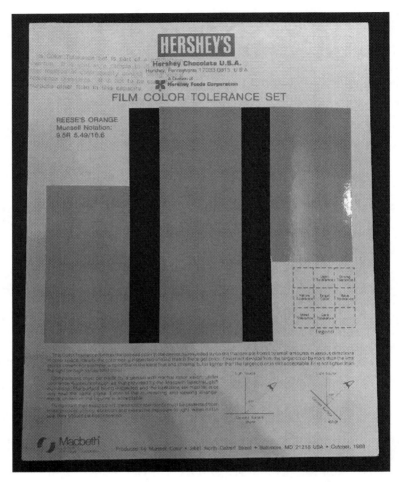

Fig. 4.6 Film color tolerance set of Hershey's Reeses produced by Macbeth (1988) (*Source* Massachusetts College of Art and Design. *Note* In October 1988, a chart was created to display the tolerance of color variation with viewing angle. The standard orange color used for Hershey's Reeses Peanut Butter Cup packaging is defined as 9.5R 5.49/16.6. At its creation, the Macbeth Company acquired the Munsell Color Company, which is why the Macbeth logo appears in the lower left corner)

CHAPTER 5

Categorizing Colors by Environment and Senses

I see your true colors and that's why I love you.
So don't be afraid to let them show your true colors.
True colors are beautiful, like a rainbow.
Cyndi Lauper, *True Colors*[1] (1986)

The English expression "true colors" means a person's real character, and people associate colors with human nature. Whether or not the inner character of a person has color, certain colors suit certain people. The colors people wear may look good or bad with their hair, skin, and eyes, and this idea is reflected in the yellow-base and blue-base analyses that have become popular for make-up and fashion. This diagnostic method was developed by Robert C. Dorr in 1928. While making theatrical posters in Chicago, he discovered that almost all colors have yellowish or bluish undertones. Undertones are the base colors, meaning that if the eyes and skin color are yellow-based, the color of cosmetics and clothing should also be yellow-based to harmonize with them. Although yellow can be taken as a warm color and blue as a cool color, this is a well-known example of a standard that divides colors that suit human appearance.

---

[1] Lyrics: Steinberg/Tom Kelly, © Sony/ATV Music Publishing LLC.

© The Author(s), under exclusive license to Springer Nature Switzerland AG 2024
K. Hidaka, *The Art of Color Categorization*,
https://doi.org/10.1007/978-3-031-47690-7_5

94   K. HIDAKA

In this chapter, I will look at the cases in which humans distinguish colors based on temperature, humidity, festive and ordinary days, and gender. In other words, warm, cool, wet, dry, festive, ordinary days, and gender will be introduced as the basis for color distinctions.

5.1   TEMPERATURE

People, even those uninterested in color theory, have probably heard the terms warm and cool in association with colors, and these are also used in Goethe's *Theory of Colors*. The perception of warmth or coolness when looking at a color is not based on its physical temperature, but rather is a psychological classification, popularized based on the empirical knowledge that many people feel warm when they see red. Another parameter, color temperature, is measured in Kelvin and does not correspond to the psychological impression of warm (red-yellow) or cool (blue-blue purple) colors.

However, green and purple are neither, or are divided into warm and cool colors in different ways by different people. In this regard, an interesting study attempted to model the cool color category by investigating color word changes from green to blue. Robert E. MacLaury, an anthropologist specializing in Central American (Mesoamerican) languages and cultures, used a procedure inherited from Berlin and Kay's *Basic Color Terms*, in which he asked approximately 900 subjects in 116 languages in Central America to name a color and indicate the focal color. The subjects were asked to name the color, indicate the focal color, and map the range of the color. According to his book *Color and Cognition in Mesoamerica: The Construction of Categories as Perspectives*[2] (1997), based on this massive survey of color words, green and blue are single-color words in Mesoamerican languages in many cases, just as they are in Japanese. The following three points were observed for green and blue focal colors and verbalization[3]:

[2] MacLaury, R. E. (1997). *Color and Cognition in Mesoamerica: Constructing Categories As Vantages.*

[3] MacLaury, R. (1997). "Skewing and Darkening: Dynamics of the Cool Category." In C. Hardin & L. Maffi (Eds), *Color Categories in Thought and Language* (pp. 261–282). Cambridge: Cambridge University Press. https://doi.org/10.1017/CBO9780511519819.012.

(1) People who speak languages that use the same word to refer to both green and blue still differentiate between cool and warm colors in the same way as those who have distinct words for green and blue. They categorize green as warm and blue as cool.

(2) When categorizing green and blue colors, dividing them into cool and not cool categories can distort or divide the boundaries of the color term category.

(3) As in (2), when classified based on whether the color is cool or not, the focal color of the color term category that was previously perceived begins to be seen as darker. With the progression of classification, a unique phenomenon was observed: the participants started to oscillate between the cool color category and the single-color name categories of green and blue, with green gradually gaining dominance and the blue focal color darkening over time compared to the green focal color.

MacLaury's classification model (1) through (3) is called the Vantage Theory and is regarded as a major achievement in the anthropological and linguistic community of color; it is a point of view on where to prioritize and focus attention to categorize colors. Humans perceive temperatures, like cool and warm, in colors. When the range of colors is divided by different conditions, humans change the focal color, range, and the name of the color they represent, distorting it accordingly. According to the results of MacLaury's experiment, when humans see the same color, if the criteria for dividing it are different, they will change the focus and the way they name it, depending on whether it is a color name or whether they perceive it as warm or cool.

What about the color division of people who speak more than one language? The Mesoamerican countries that MacLaury examined are regions with many bilingual speakers of Mesoamerican languages and Spanish. Spanish categorizes green and blue into different categories. Mesoamerican bilingual speakers use the Mesoamerican language color categories and the Spanish color categories differently, just as they use different ways of dividing temperature and color names.

The changes in bilingual speakers' way of naming and viewing colors as their acquired languages increase have been studied as far back as Lenneberg and Roberts (see Chapter 3); more recent scholars include MacLaury, Andrews, Loitšenko, and Winawer. Evolutionary biologist Henrich sees this as evolution and explains that language acquisition

96 K. HIDAKA

changes various aspects of the human psyche and gives individuals cognitive abilities they did not have before.[4] Those who lean towards linguistic relativism, such as Henrich, view multilingualism as an expansion of cognitive abilities.

I must admit that I had some doubts about Henrich's commentary. I speak English and Japanese, having lived in the US and the UK. However, my ability to perceive color does not change based on my language. Regardless of which language I speak, what I see is still the same landscape, but I speak it as a different categorization. On the other hand, I am surprised when I see different coloring in landscapes outside Japan. However, I do not know if the change whereby I gradually become accustomed to the coloring is the expansion of cognitive abilities described by Henrich—or evolution.

5.2 HUMIDITY

A well-known study in the cultural anthropology of color categorization rooted in the natural environment and climate, mentioned in Lévi-Strauss's *La Pensée Sauvage,* comes from the Hanunóo people of the Philippines.

The Hanunóo, slash-and-burn farming people of southern Mindoro, Philippines, have four color categories: light, dark, dry, and wet. In his article "Hanunóo Color Categories,"[5] Harold Colyer Conklin, a cultural anthropologist specializing primarily in the Philippines, identified three attributes (hue, lightness, and saturation) and warm and cool colors as different classifications. Conklin was the first to introduce this Hanunóo example to Western societies as a standard for classification different from the Western triad.

(* *ma* is the Hanunóo prefix for "represent, have.")

(1) *Brightness (ma)lagti*
Refers to white and high brightness and the combination of these colors.

---

[4] Henrich, J. (2015). *The Secret of Our Success: How Culture Is Driving Human Evolution, Domesticating Our Species, and Making Us Smarter* (Imanishi Y., Trans.). Hakuyosha, pp. 385–386.

[5] Conklin, H. C. (1955). Hanunóo Color Categories. *Southwestern Journal of Anthropology*, 11(4), pp. 339–344.

5 CATEGORIZING COLORS BY ENVIRONMENT AND SENSES 97

(2) *Darkness* **(ma)biru**
Broadly refers to black, purple, indigo, blue, dark green, dark gray, and other low-light hues.

(3) *General term for reddish color* **(ma)rara**
A mixture of maroon (dark red, chestnut), red, orange, yellow, or similar colors. It means not merely redness but also dryness. Yellowed bamboo or ripe corn is called *(ma)rara*.

(4) *General term for colors with greenish tints* (**ma**)*latuy*
Light green, mixed with green, yellow, and light brown (also means "glossy and fresh." Conklin analogizes that the word is used because living plants are green and contain moisture.)

At first, Conklin asked the Hanunóo to name the colors while showing them scattered cards and clothes. Conklin could not understand their answers because they sounded contradictory, for example referring to the same hue by different color names. However, when the colors were contrasted, they all agreed on the same classification. When he asked the reason for the contrasting classifications, Conklin's doubts were clarified.[6] The Mindoro province of the Philippines, where the Hanunóo people live, is tropical, with only two seasons, wet and dry, rather than the four seasons of spring, summer, fall, and winter, as in Japan and temperate and subtropical zones. However, as in Japan and temperate zones, the day is 24 hours long, with bright days and dark nights. Day and night and the seasons have created a Hanunóo worldview in which colors are classified as light/dark and dry/wet.

When the Hanunóo and others look at color, they are not simply concerned with the appearance of the color, but also focus on the texture. The same tree leaf has a different texture in the dry season, with its withered feel, compared to its wet, life-like freshness in the rainy season. This perspective of dry and wet also influences the Hanunóo people's sense of beauty. For example, if there are green beads and red beads, the green color is considered of higher quality. This is because green is considered fresh, and red is considered dead. The appearance of a pigment or dye color can vary greatly depending on the material and texture to which it is applied. For instance, color may appear differently on shiny, rough, uneven fabric, paint, ceramics, and other surfaces. Similarly, for

---

[6] Lévi-Strauss. (1976). *La Pensée Sauvage* (Japanese translation), p. 66.

98 K. HIDAKA

the Hanunóo people, colors that have not faded and are full of life (fresh and not withered) are considered of a higher value. The criteria for high-end or low-end colors differ from one ethnic group to another, and this is an incentive to diversify aesthetic sensibilities and values.

The above four classifications of the Hanunóo are considered typical examples of cultural relativism and have tended to be used to reinforce linguistic relativism. The Hanunóo index of color categorization is fundamentally different from those generalized in the Western world, as it is based on the logic of dry and rainy seasons. It seems ethnocentric to assume that warm and cool colors, or the three attributes of hue, lightness, and saturation generalized in the Western world, are the only correct criteria for color categorization.

As we saw in Chapter 3, certain ethnocentric theories have supported *Basic Color Terms*. One such theory posits that societies near the equator primarily use color words to differentiate only lightness (lightness/darkness).[7] At the same time, people closer to the North and South Poles, on the contrary, are primarily conscious of hue and lightness. This claim by Van Wijk from a linguistic and ethnographic perspective was documented in *Basic Color Terms* as evidence supporting Berlin and Kay's evolutionary model. Berlin and Kay imply that white and black are color words for light and dark contrasts and that the languages of peri-equatorial regions are light/dark-centered and have fewer color names, while languages from temperate zones are light and hue-centered; therefore, the color names of temperate-zone languages are more developed.[8] The Hanunóo language, spoken in the equatorial periphery, uniquely categorizes colors based on dry and wet textures. This system has developed over time in a two-season environment. The Hanunóo color categorization exhibits a comprehension and articulation of dryness and moisture that is superior to Western color attributes.

It is crucial to acknowledge that the systems of categorizing colors based on hue, lightness, and saturation by Munsell and the color scale introduced by Ostwald (black and white, pure and mixed colors) were solely developed within Western society. The fact that these systems are

---

[7] Berlin, B., & Kay, P. (1969). *Basic Color Terms*, pp. 149–150. Van Wijk. (1959). A Cross-Cultural Theory of Colour and Brightness Nomenclature.

[8] Berlin, B., & Kay, P. (1969). *Basic Color Terms*, pp. 149–150.

based on Western cultural norms implies that they may not be universally applicable across different cultures and may not represent the diverse color categorizations that exist worldwide. Furthermore, the Munsell color chart, which converts a three-dimensional color space into a two-dimensional one for convenience, cannot represent all colors that exist, and it must exclude texture.

Is using the Munsell color chart, the American color standard, intrinsically valid? Belgian social anthropologist Saunders raised this question in response to Berlin and Kay's survey in 1995.[9] Saunders, who leaned toward linguistic relativism, questioned whether the method of presenting a flat Munsell color chart of three attributes as a stimulus would hinder the discovery of new standards and varieties of color categorization. Philosopher Jaap van Brakel, also of the Catholic University of Leuven like Sanders, continued the argument against the foundation of how the BCT was determined.[10] The argument is that using criteria determined by American logic (Munsell's color chart and the BCT prerequisites) to investigate the logic of other languages is a fundamental mistake.

What form of survey color stimulus or color chart should be used to investigate color categorization? Indeed, the three attributes are a way of dividing colors as determined by the American Munsell. Since Munsell died at the beginning of the twentieth century and the Munsell Color Company is no longer in existence, we cannot ask for the official opinion of the manufacturer.

Is it better to use someone else's standardized listing, such as the Munsell color chart used for the survey by Lenneberg and Roberts, Berlin and Kay, and others, or is it better to divide the color chart into individual chips, as Kuriki et al. did? (see Chapter 3, Sect. 3.2). If we want to investigate where the boundaries between colors are, perhaps we should show a continuous color listing sheet with no scale or dividing lines drawn. On the other hand, if we want to investigate why informants are so particular about their categorization, it may be better to have them categorize random individual color chips or cards rather than a list-type chart. Color sorting and category research tools will likely be areas for further study.

[9] Saunders, B. (1995). "Disinterring Basic Color Terms: A Study in the Mystique of Cognitivism." *History of the Human Sciences*, 8(4), pp. 19–38.

[10] Saunders, B. A. C., & Van Brakel, J. (2001). "Rewriting Color." *Philosophy of the Social Sciences*, 31(4), pp. 538–556.

5.3 Domestic Animals

Humans develop a sense of color by looking at familiar colors and understanding others with similar living environments. For example, the Bodi people of Nile origin who live in southwestern Ethiopia use the familiar domesticated cattle as a standard for color categorization. The Bodi recognize the colors and patterns of cattle, and their color categorization system is based on the color of cattle.[11] This is an example of a group that is particular about what they value in their daily lives, and this becomes the basis for their classification system.

Anthropologist Katsuyoshi Fukui investigated the classification of color in the Bodi people, based on previous studies of the Hanunóo people by Conklin and the color languages of Berlin and Kay. Fukui conducted his survey twice. The first time, he used 202 color cards, and the second time he used 98 color cards and had the subjects call the cards by their color names and explain what kind of color they were. The cards used in the first survey were the 202 color cards[12] given to Fukui by Turton, a British anthropologist who had previously conducted research in Ethiopia. The second survey was based on Color Scheme (A): 98 High-Quality Standard Colors (1975), supervised by the General Japan Color Research Institute. Fukui narrowed down the number of cards to 98 after reflecting that the 202 color cards used in the first survey were too numerous.[13] In Conklin's survey of the four Hanunóo tribal taxa described in the previous section, great results were achieved using color cards rather than color charts and having the participants sort randomly placed items according to their cultural criteria. In an inquiry about cultural criteria and values, i.e., for what reasons to categorize them, random color cards may be the best choice. However, as Fukui's reflections suggest, too many choices in the number of cards may present problems for the subjects. If they are given too many choices, it may be more difficult for people to name and categorize the cards.

---

[11] Fukui, K. (1991). *Recognition and Culture: An Ethnography of Color and Pattern*, p. 165.

[12] Fukui, K. (1991). *Recognition and Culture: An Ethnography of Color and Pattern*, p. 22.

[13] Fukui, K. (1991). *Recognition and Culture: An Ethnography of Color and Pattern*, p. 42. The General Japan Color Research Institute described by Fukui no longer exist, and its cards are not sold.

The survey revealed that the Bodi people have eight BCT terms: *goroni* (red), *nyagazi* (orange), *shimaji* (purple), *chai* (yellow-green to green-blue category), *birezi* (yellow), *gidagi* (gray), *hori* (white), and *koro* (black).[14] From the color card survey, Fukui found that for the Bodi people, variations in the color of cattle hair are the main source of color words and that hair patterns are regarded in the same way as colors, collectively known as *aegi* (a compound concept of color and hair pattern).[15]

Cattle are vital to the Bodi people for food, hides, and labor. The colors of Ethiopian wild cattle are very diverse, with green, blue, and yellow cattle. The frontispiece of Fukui's *Recognition and Culture* includes a picture of a blue (bluish-gray) cow. The Bodi people have identified more than 60 types of these richly colored cows and have verbalized the hues and patterns, forming an aegis. The Bodi people observed cattle, and "all the colors and patterns that exist as the epidermis of cattle"[16] have names and are the source of the Bodi language's most significant categorization standards and color names.

Conversely, colors and patterns that do not exist as the color of the epidermis of cattle do not have names. The cow is also the standard when considering color similarities. *Goroni* (red) and *nyagazi* (orange) are placed in the same category of *ganiya* (blood relation). This is because *goroni* and *nyagazi* directly related to the mating of cows, and a cow with a *goroni* coat color and a cow with *nyagazi* coat color belong to the same *kabchotch* (type), as they are considered as such.

In Japan and many other societies, cattle are raised exclusively as dairy or beef breeds. As a result of only breeding cattle that are convenient for Japanese livelihoods, black, brown, or black-and-white cows are the overwhelming majority, and blue or yellow cows are culled. Thus, cow color is not a standard for representing a variety of colors. A phenomenon similar to this unification of cattle colors can be recalled in the case of carrots. Carrots originally came from Afghanistan; the original species were purple and brown. However, mainly orange carrots were grown worldwide as a

---

[14] Fukui, K. (1991). *Recognition and Culture: An Ethnography of Color and Pattern*, pp. 66–67.

[15] Fukui, K. (1978). 'Color' and 'Pattern' of the Bodi People: The World of Pastoralists, Southwest Ethiopia. In *The Symbolic World of Color and Pattern in Pastoral Society: The Bodi People of Ethiopia*, pp. 36–49, 48–79.

[16] Ibid.

symbol of respect to the Dutch royal family of Orange (Huis van Oranje-Nassau). Thus carrot = orange became established in Japan and Europe, according to a folklore theory.[17] As a result of artificially biased breeding and cultivation, the variation of colors in the environment was reduced.

While this is a slight digression from the topic of classification by cattle, let me introduce an interesting color culture among the Bodi people called "morale" in addition to the use of cattle as a standard for color. When the Bodi people grow up, they have their own morale, which can be described as their color and pattern.[18] Morale symbolizes colors and patterns associated with animals, insects, and plants around them, and they decide on their morale. They have a strong attachment and commitment to the identity of the exclusive colors, animals, patterns, etc. that they have decided upon as their morale.[19] For example, a girl who chose her morale as red (*goroni* in Bodi = metaphor for dragonfly) was so impressed by the vividness of the red color card Fukui showed her that she cried with joy.[20] Perhaps she was not accustomed to seeing the color of artificial printing ink, but she was moved to see the beautifully colored printed red as her color once again.

The concept of color is just one of the properties of some objects reflected in the light. The reason why dyes and flowers in Japanese and pigments of paints, minerals, animals, and foods in English tend to be the origin of color words is that we perceive variations of colors in these things. Each language gives detailed names and classifications to those parts of its living environment that it is particular about, as in the case of Japan, which describes in detail the changes in the environment of the four seasons, is surrounded by the sea, and has many names for fish. What the multitude of color words are derived from, and the criteria used to categorize colors indicate what the language speaker is particular about. Furthermore, the example of the Bodi tribe's morale clearly shows diversity in how people are particular about and attached to color itself.

[17] https://www.livescience.com/why-are-carrots-orange.html (Accessed: May 10, 2021).

[18] https://www.afrospace.info/Ethiopia-Bodi.htm (Accessed: Feb. 27, 2021).

[19] Fukui, K. (1991). *Recognition and Culture: An Ethnography of Color and Pattern*, pp. 171–176.

[20] Fukui, K. (1991). *Recognition and Culture: An Ethnography of Color and Pattern*, p. 179.

5.4 Festivals and Everyday Life

Celebrations and noncelebrations also occupy an important place as standards for color categorization. In Japan, the basic colors for celebration are red and white; pink is also used. Red and white, gold and silver, and gold and red are used for celebrations. Conversely, for misfortunes, white, indigo and white, and black and white are used.[21] Similar achromatic colors, like gray and navy blue, are often used for noncelebrations. Today, black is considered the color of mourning for non-festive celebrations, but before World War II, relatives wore white. The colors used for longevity celebrations are red for *Kanreki* (60th birthday) and *Beiju* (88th birthday), yellow for *Koki* (70th birthday), purple for *Kiju* (77th birthday), and white for *Hakuju* (99th birthday).

Although symbolic colors for festive and non-festive occasions vary somewhat from country to country, it is common in many countries that people generally follow occasional conventions of color when wrapping and decorating goods and money. Color is a metaphor for social events, as explained by Katsuyoshi Fukui.[22] Halloween and Christmas decorations in the US are orange/black and red/green, respectively. Interestingly, Halloween has also taken root in Japan since the end of the twentieth century. Although the skin color of pumpkin varieties growing in Japan is not originally orange like in the United States, bright orange is used for jack-o-lantern decorations and costume goods. This is a curious case in which the color of a plant associated with a foreign event has become widespread, even though it is the color of a variety not widely grown in Japan.

The colors of social events can be divided into *hare* (celebration) versus *ke* (mundane), categories rediscovered by the Japanese folklorist and bureaucrat Yanagita Kunio.[23] The literal translation of *hare* is "a clear, sunny day." The literal translation of *ke* is "usual." A 17th-century Jesuit is believed to have first discovered the contrasting relationship between *hare* and *ke* in Japan. The concept was described in *the Vocabulary of*

---

[21] In Japan's Kansai (Western) area, yellow is also used for funeral decorations.

[22] Fukui, K. (1991). *Recognition and Culture: An Ethnography of Color and Pattern*, p. 39.

[23] Hidaka, K. (2017). "Categorization of Japanese Traditional Color Scheme into 'Hare-Ke': An Attempt from View of Food Culture." *Journal of the Color Science Association of Japan*, 41(3+), pp. 34–35.

the *Japanese and Portuguese Language*, published by the Jesuits at that time. *Hare* refers to great festivals, such as annual events, rites of passage, weddings, and funerals, while *ke* refers to everyday life and quotidian labor. The etymology of *hare* refers to clear skies, indicating a bright state of mind. *Ke* is said to lead to *kegare*, indicating a dark state. *Hare* and *ke* have often been compared to the French sociologist Émile Durkheim's dualism of the sacred and the secular. Durkheim attempted to identify the seasonal alternating rhythms of dry-season labor (secular) and rainy-season rituals (sacred) in tribal societies in Central Australia as the genesis of sacred-secular dualism.[24] During the rainy season, hunting and gathering are not allowed outdoors, so rituals and festivals are exclusively held indoors, and everyone celebrates with delicious treats. As with the Hanunóo, this worldview is born from a two-season environment: the rainy and dry seasons. Unlike the dualism of sacred and secular, Japanese *hare* and *ke* are divided only by the presence or absence of a sense of routine in the rhythm of life rather than by sacredness or secularity. Table 5.1 shows how the colors of *hare* and *ke* are classified in Japan.

Just as Australian tribal societies feast during festive seasons, Japan also has special meals for *hare* (festive) occasions. *Hare* foods and drinks are special foodstuffs called *kawarimono*, which include sake, fish, rice, rice cakes, sweets, meat, and sushi. In *hare*, rice is featured as an ingredient

Table 5.1 Comparison of hare and ke color schemes

		Hare	Ke
Mainly used colors	Hue	Red and white, five colors, seven colors, gold and silver, brocade	Blue, green, brown, gray, black
	Value (lightness)	High	Low
	Chroma (saturation)	High	Low
Forms of Social Events	Tonality of items	Multicolored	Similar hues
	Labor	Time-consuming	Easy and casual
	Frequency	Once a year; once a life	Weekday

[24] Shimada, H. (2016). "The Age of One Man's Religion." *History of Religious Events as a Culture.*

and dumplings, rice cakes, and sake are served. The most representative *hare* festive food is New Year's *osechi*, an abbreviation of *osechi-ryori*, which derives from the Chinese Five Seasonal Festivals. There is no New Year's cuisine concept in most of Europe, the Middle East, and Africa. However, food culture related to religious events, such as Christmas and Ramadan, is inseparable from daily life.

During Japan's Edo period (1603–1868), there was a custom of offering brightly colored "seven-colored sweets" on the 57th day of the sexagenary cycle. The seven-color confections of Mogi Honke in Nagasaki, founded in 1844, are an assortment of red, white, green, and blue candies, and *rakugan,* a dry confection of starch and sugar, dyed with food colorants and shaped like lucky charms, such as cranes, turtles, and sea bream.[25] The seven colors mean many kinds of colors, symbolizing the custom of using many colors for special occasions. In Japan, seven colors were a word meaning "many colors," as in the expression "seven colors change." Colorful foods are typical of *hare*.

At times of *hare*, which is categorized by annual *hare* events repeated every year, i.e., rites of passage in a person's life (marriage, birth, funeral), foods different from those consumed in everyday life are served. Despite being a foreign custom, wedding cakes appear at weddings as a matter of course in modern Japan. Funeral buns (often white and yellow, but there is no rule) are given to mourners in return, as a gesture to mean returning the deceased's property in a form that will please them.

Yanagita theorized that the distinction between *hare* and *ke* in food is not the price or quality of the ingredients, but the labor involved in making them.[26] Until the modern era, the usual diet consisted of one soup and one meal, with only a little time and effort spent refining and cooking *ke* foods. The main ingredients of daily *ke* food were unrefined barley, brown rice, millet, nuts, potatoes, buckwheat, etc. As a result, the color scheme of *ke* food tends to be low in brightness. Seasonings, broths, and other sober colors are common; few foods use coloring. The standard color scheme uses bright red (e.g., red ginger) and a small amount of green (*baran*, decorative greens for sushi and sashimi) as accent colors. Japan has an unspoken rule for this kind of color scheme.

---

[25] https://mogi105.com/c-item-detail?ic=0016-01 (Accessed Feb. 27, 2021).

[26] Taniguchi, M. (1989). "Yanagita Kunio's *Hare-Ke* Theory." *New Collection of Japanese Literature Research Materials*, 29, Yuseido, pp. 62–77.

With the modernization and economic development of Japan, diets have changed, leading to a broader range of beverages and food items, including alcohol, meat, fish, and confectionery, becoming more accessible and common. With advances in agricultural technology and the availability of imported foods, we now have access to a wider variety of foods throughout the year. As a result, seasonal foods have become less common. The influence of foreign events, customs, tableware, and eating habits has also changed our food's color schemes. In modern times, sushi and cakes have become more popular. Additionally, more Japanese people now celebrate Western events like Christmas, Halloween, and Easter, which has blurred the distinctions between festivals and everyday life. This blurring of the boundaries between *hare* and *ke* and seasonality in daily life may change the traditional Japanese view of color in the future.[27]

5.5 GENDER

The combination of red and white has been used as the color of *hare*, but it is also related to gender. In Japan, there is a classification of colors by gender, called men's colors and women's colors.[28] In the NHK *Kōhaku Uta Gassen* broadcast which occurs every New Year's Eve, male singers and hosts are divided into the white group and female singers and hosts into the red group.

There was a tradition that cool colors (blue and navy blue) and achromatic colors (white and black) were the colors for boys, while warm colors, especially red and pink, were the colors for girls. Color gendering exists, as in with the phrase "pink is for girls, blue is for boys."[29] Pink has a very strong conceptual association with women and is a color that represents gender stereotypes, as found in a survey of American college

---

[27] Hidaka, K. (2017). "Categorization of Japanese Traditional Color Scheme into 'Hare-Ke': An Attempt from View of Food Culture." *Journal of the Color Science Association of Japan*, 41(3+), pp. 34–35.

[28] Hoshino, S. (2011). "Section 5.4: Color and Gender in Four Cities in Three Nordic Countries (& Paris)," Mitsuboshi, M. (Ed.), *Color Symbols of the World: Aspects of Nature, Language, and Culture*. pp. 292–298.

[29] Boyatzis & Varghese (1994). Kitagami, S., et al. (2010). Does Color Matter for Toilet Marks? (2) A Comparative Cultural Examination of Stroop-like Effects in the Recognition of Toilet Marks, p. 28.

5 CATEGORIZING COLORS BY ENVIRONMENT AND SENSES   107

students' perceptions of bathroom marks conducted by cognitive psychologist Shinji Kitagami and colleagues.[30] In this study, the Stroop effect was observed by respondents in male toilet marks colored pink. The Stroop effect/interference is a phenomenon in which people feel uncomfortable with the semantic information of a letter or mark.

The superimposition of images of women in red and pink colors is largely due to the influence of the media. In the musical film *Funny Face* (1957), starring Audrey Hepburn, a scene in which she sings and dances to the song "Think Pink!" suggests that female dresses and shoes, for adults and children, be pink. There is a scene where the women wear pink, and the men wear white. Also, in the American romantic film *Pretty in Pink* (1986), as the title suggests, the main character, a high school girl, wears a pink dress to a high school prom. The boys in formal attire at the prom wear white or black suits. Many films made in the twentieth century promoted the notion that pink is a female color and achromatic colors and blue are male colors. These films may have imprinted gender stereotypes on their viewers.

Since 2006, the World Economic Forum has published the Global Gender Gap Report,[31] a ranking that visualizes equality and inequality by gender in countries around the world. Based on this, the movement to eliminate disparities based on gender has accelerated throughout the world. As a result, the separation of colors by gender is becoming rare pan-globally,[32] but there are still many instances in signs for Japanese restrooms and public bathhouses where black and blue are for men and red is for women.

When humans began to color-code by gender is a mystery, but we can speculate on the basis for color-coding. It is universal that humans are born either physically male or female. Here is an example of color-coding based on physical gender with symbolism and color-coding by the Ndembu people of Zambia and Zimbabwe, located in Central Africa. A Scottish cultural anthropologist, Victor Witter Turner, identified white, red, and black as the basic colors used in Ndembu ceremonies.[33] Turner

---

[30] Kitagami, S., et al. (2010). Does Color Matter for Toilet Marks? (2) A Comparative Cultural Examination of Stroop-like Effects in the Recognition of Toilet Marks, p. 28.

[31] In 2020, Japan's gender gap index ranks 121st among 153 countries.

[32] Gender-neutral toilets are becoming more common worldwide, with the norm being signs without categorization by color.

[33] Turner, V. (1967). *The Forest of Symbols: Aspects of the Ndembu Ritual*, pp. 59–74.

is credited with popularizing the cultural anthropological term *liminality* and, in his studies of Ndembu rites of passage and religious ceremonies, he referred to people who are on the margins, away from the norms of everyday life, as liminal.[34] Liminality is derived from the Latin word *limen*, meaning threshold. This classification division by liminality has some similarities to the classification of *hare* and *ke*.

As we saw in Chapter 2, white and black are the first stage in the evolutionary model of Berlin and Kay's BCTs. Red is the second stage and is considered the BCT recognized from the beginning. Many cultures believe these three colors represent the minimum basic human need for color. Turner found that the red and white clay and black charcoal used in the Ndembu ritual had symbolic meanings.[35]

Red and white are treated as a pair,[36] representing duality, with white being associated with masculinity and red with femininity. Turner explains that white is associated with the color of semen and red with the color of blood in childbirth and menstruation.[37] Wierzbicka, an authority on semantics, points out that the word red is often derived from blood or fire. This association between biological sex and color seems common and universal, as in Japan, where red and white (female and male) indicate pairs.

The symbolism of the colors of the Ndembu people, placed in the highest opposition, is the contrast between white and black (life and death).[38] Some colors symbolize life and death—the part of life we must pass through as long as we have life.

The concept of *communitas*, introduced by Turner, is also interesting. The term refers to belonging to a community of people who have gone through a common experience or rite of passage. A sense of camaraderie among people with similar experiences is common among people other than the Ndembu.

---

[34] In a rite of passage, for example, participants are said to stand on the threshold between their previous state of identity, time, or community belonging and the new state established by the completion of the rite.

[35] Turner, V. (1967). *The Forest of Symbols: Aspects of the Ndembu Ritual*, pp. 59–74.

[36] Turner, V. (1967). *The Forest of Symbols: Aspects of the Ndembu Ritual*, p. 79.

[37] Turner, V. (1967). *The Forest of Symbols: Aspects of the Ndembu Ritual*, p. 61.

[38] Deflem, M. (1991). Ritual, Anti-Structure, and Religion: A Discussion of Victor Turner's Processual Symbolic Analysis, pp. 1–25.

Thus far, examples of humans distinguishing colors based on their environment and senses have been shown. The author hopes that readers understand that if we live as human beings on earth, only phenomena and concepts commonly understood by the members of each culture should be the basis for color distinctions. In particular, the common basis of the senses that constitute a society, such as the difference in brightness between day and night, the difference in seasons, and the colors associated with everyday life and extraordinary life, physical gender, life, and death, are likely to be the criteria that govern each person's worldview.

5.6 Synesthetes

Synesthesia is a unique perceptual phenomenon in which one sensory stimulus causes both its sense and another sense simultaneously. This is called multimodal, and the phenomenon of multiple simultaneous sensory responses has been studied in psychology. Many synesthesia cases are related to colors, such as color and sound, color and taste, and color and shape or letter. Kandinsky described the association between color and the sound of musical instruments[39] (see Chapter 2, Sect. 2.2). Sound–color synesthesia (color hearing) is a form of synesthesia in which an individual hears sounds while looking at colors. For example, upon seeing the color red, the sound of a piano is heard.

Synesthesia is said to be relatively common among artists. Music producer, singer, and fashion designer Pharrell Williams (1973–), who has won 13 Grammy Awards, has publicly described himself as a synesthete.[40] Among historical musicians, Scriabin and Rimsky-Korsakov were possible synesthetes. Franz Liszt, Kenji Miyazawa, Nabokov, and Stevie Wonder are among the famous people who are believed to have synesthesia.

The perceived content of synaesthesia was considered individualized by synaesthetes, but studies have found commonalities in experiments with many subjects. For example, a group experiment with synaesthesia holders who heard sounds with colors found that the higher the sound, the

---

[39] Kandinsky. (1912). *Concerning the Spiritual in Art*, Bijutsu Shuppansha, Japanese translation in 1958.

[40] McComb, L. (2012). Pharrell William's Extraordinary Gift. *The Oprah Magazine*, October.

110 K. HIDAKA

brighter the color tended to appear. Similarly, a group experiment with grapheme–color synesthesia holders, who sometimes saw black letters as a different color, found that they tended to perceive similar colors for certain letters. The range of senses that correspond to colors, sounds, numbers, concepts, and tastes is wide. The variety makes objectively defining and sharing the synesthesia possessed by individuals difficult.

There are many different types of synesthesia, each with its own specific sensory pairings. The following are typical phenomena of color synaesthesia, but there is room for future discoveries of other combinations.

> *Synesthesia with letter ⇄ color vision*
> *Sound ⇄ Color vision synesthesia is called color hearing*
> *Taste ⇄ Color*
> *Texture, hardness ⇄ , and color*
> *Scent ⇄ Color*
> *a person's personality, appearance ⇄, and color*
> *Time unit ⇄ color vision synesthesia*
> *Number ⇄ Color visible synesthesia synesthetes who see color in numbers, but who "see" no change in color in the eyes of Chinese numbers or dice, perceive color in the size of the number.*

Recently, I saw a Twitter post (@nmd_mnd, 2019— 10–28, Twitter) in which a father and son who seem to have synesthesia often mistakenly add $5 + 3 = 7$. They feel that 5 is dark green and 3 is yellow; thus, the added color is a yellow-green seven. Also surprising is that parents and children feel the same color. I cannot imagine such a miscalculation because I do not see any color in numbers.

However, when I was an adjunct instructor at an art college, after a class explaining synesthesia, I said, "Ever since I was a little girl, I have always been able to see the do-re-mi-fa-so-la-ti 123456, and whenever I see or hear a letter of the alphabet, I always see a color. As a kid, it was hard to get frustrated when I saw colors like 4 = green and 4 = red. I've gotten over it now, though." One anonymous student said, "I'm unsure if this is true. I suspect that this person also has genuine synesthesia."

Others cannot understand synaesthesia unless the individual communicates their worldview. A poem by the symbolist Arthur Rimbaud (1854–1891), cited as a staple in the literature on synesthesia, contains a synesthetic description of seeing colors in letters.

5 CATEGORIZING COLORS BY ENVIRONMENT AND SENSES 111

Voyalles (1871)

Black A, white E, red I, green U, blue O: you vowels,
Someday I'll tell the tale of where your mystery lies:
Black A, a jacket formed of hairy, shiny flies
That buzz among harsh stinks in the abyss's bowels;

White E, the white of kings, of moon-washed fogs and tents,
Of fields of shivering chervil, glaciers' gleaming tips;
Red I, magenta, spat-up blood, the curl of lips
In laughter, hatred, or besotted penitence;

Green U, vibrating waves in viridescent seas,
Or peaceful pastures flecked with beasts – furrows of peace
Imprinted on our brows as if by alchemies;

Blue O, great Trumpet blaring strange and piercing cries
Through Silences where Worlds and Angels pass crosswise;
Omega, O, the violet brilliance of Those Eyes!
Arthur Rimbaud, translated by George J. Dance

A film based on the true story of a synaesthete is *The Soloist* (2009). The film tells the story of Nathaniel Anthony Ayers, Jr. (1951–), a music prodigy who attended the prestigious Juilliard School in New York and had a promising future but became mentally ill and homeless, and the journalist who attempted to support him. In the film is a scene in which Ayers, while listening to music, begins to see dancing-colored lights and then experiences confusion symptoms. When an individual has a worldview different from the majority, such as synesthesia, it is difficult to share and gain understanding with others. A unique worldview can easily be considered socially deviant, but a part of it becomes more socially acceptable under the name of "art." An eternal mystery is whether the colors reflected in an individual's worldview can be accurately shared with others.

PART II

Categorizing Things 'by' Color

CHAPTER 6

Categorizing Food by Color

Isn't it barbaric to judge another country's food culture as barbaric just because it differs from your own?
Shiro Yamaoka, Whale Fighting, *Oishinbo a la Carte 13.*[1]

Shiro Yamaoka, the main character of the Japanese comic book *Oishinbo a la Carte*, has this to say to foreigners who are negative about whale-eating culture: it is common for people to feel offended by negative comments about the food they eat; other people's rejection of food that is different from our traditional food culture (i.e., barbaric), which is like a spinal reflex, can lead to confrontation. Moreover, there are many religious and ethical restrictions, prohibitions, and conflicting opinions on eating different meats such as pork, beef, whale flesh and fat, horses, dogs, and even foie gras, so that fundamental understanding among them is complex.

In the Introduction, I described my experience of being surprised by the vivid colors of food, especially cakes, when I first lived in the United States. I see now that my rejection was of the certain artificiality and toxicity I felt in the bright colors of American cakes at that time. In general, though, during my years living in the United States, I gradually

---

[1] Kariya, T., & Hanasaki, A. (1987). *Oishinbo a la Carte 13.* Shogakukan, p. 37.

© The Author(s), under exclusive license to Springer Nature Switzerland AG 2024
K. Hidaka, *The Art of Color Categorization*,
https://doi.org/10.1007/978-3-031-47690-7_6

115

Fig. 6.1 Rainbow cookies, US East Coast

became accustomed to the environment, and learned to put a comfortable distance between myself and the differences and to look at them objectively.

On the East Coast of the US, there is a rainbow-colored layer cake called a rainbow cookie, commonly eaten by people of Jewish, Eastern European and Italian descent[2] (Fig. 6.1). It is said that Jewish immigrants to the United States around 1920 first popularized rainbow cookies, and now they are one of the sweets that celebrate the Jewish holiday of Passover. I grew up seeing these brightly colored cakes in Jewish bakeries (*kosher* or *kasher*) in and around New York City. A similarly colorful cake, the Neapolitan cake made by people of Italian descent, combines a tri-colored sponge (white from vanilla, brown from chocolate, and pink from strawberries) with a sweet, creamy buttercream. Sometimes, the chocolate portion is green to represent the Italian tricolor flag. From the three colors of the Neapolitan cake, the rainbow cookie appears to have evolved to six or seven colors. Through a comparison between Japan and the United States, I here analyze the differences in the use of color in food culture and how we divide our lives "by color."

[2] https://en.wikipedia.org/wiki/rainbow_cookie.

6.1 Package 1: Milk in the USA and Japan

At what age do people build and solidify their stereotypes of color and appetite? I have focused on milk as the cornerstone of these stereotypes because milk is consumed worldwide as one of the complete nutritional foods. Therefore, I hypothesized that color, which humans see daily from infancy, might be one of the roots of color culture, and I conducted research accordingly. Milk itself is white, but its packaging uses a variety of hues. Motoko Hayakawa, a researcher in human developmental sciences, identified that white, blue, red, and yellow-green are commonly used on milk cartons in Japan,[3] and a student at Tama Art University observed that milk cartons are often white and blue or white and green.[4] I investigated if these color patterns hold across Japan, and, if so, whether they are a common phenomenon in other countries as well. For milk, a geographic comparison between the United States and Japan is the ideal approach to compare carton colors, as the milk content colors are quite similar in both countries.

Food packaging is not only a container for transportation and storage but also a sales promotion tool and a medium that concretely reflects each country's ethnicity and food culture. Packaging is a silent salesman, said Louis Cheskin (1907–1981), an authority on color science and a packaging consultant.[5] People trust appearances and consume products that have attractive packaging.

For this study, I acquired milk cartons made of paper from different dairy manufacturers in Japan (Tokyo, Chiba, and Kanagawa prefectures = Kanto area, and Sapporo, Hokkaido) and the United States between May and August of 2015. Plastic containers are not commonly used for large-volume milk in Japan, unlike in the United States. In my research, I specifically examined various types of milk, including whole, high-fat, low-fat, fat-free, and lactose-free. I made sure to exclude any milk with

---

[3] Hayakawa, M. (2000). Color Image of Milk Packages of Various Companies–Symbolism of Color. *Sanno University Bulletin*, pp. 333–334.

[4] Tama Art University, Faculty of Art and Design, "Color Planning Theory" Assignment Report, 2015, p. 1.

[5] Ibuki, T. (2005). *110 Articles of Package Strategy <Part 1>*. Nippo Shuppan, p. 17.

packaging using colors indicative of its flavor, like brown for chocolate milk or pink for strawberry milk.[6]

I obtained a total of 80 milk cartons for this research: 40 from supermarkets and convenience stores in the Kanto area; 20 from Sapporo, Hokkaido (these were mailed to relatives living in Sapporo); and 20 obtained locally in the United States. I created a chart of all 80 milk cartons to compare the differences in color schemes.[7] From this survey, I identified the overwhelming use of white in milk packaging in both the United States and the Kanto area and Sapporo in Japan, followed by the heavy use of blue, red, and blue-green to green hues. Notably, there was some distinction between the shades of white in the two countries; specifically, in the milk packaging in the United States, there was a slight shade of yellow (Fig. 6.2).

Conversely, in decreasing frequency, the least used colors for milk packaging were purple, gray, yellow, and blue-purple. Furthermore, yellow was rarely used in Japan but was often used in US designs as an accent color, especially in banners for emphasis. Separately, even though white

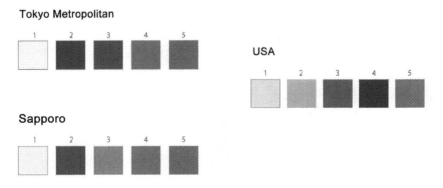

Fig. 6.2 Top 1–5 typical colors used for milk cartons

---

[6] Hidaka, K. (2015). A Comparative Cultural Study of Milk Carton Color Schemes and Designs in the U.S. and Japan. *Tama Art University Bulletin*, (30), pp. 155–163.

[7] I captured images of 40 milk cartons and converted them into digital format. Then, I used Adobe Color CC for color measurement and to extract the colors. Next, I utilized Adobe Illustrator to organize the extracted colors into 10 Munsell hues: red, orange, yellow, yellow-green, green, blue-green, blue, blue-violet, purple, and red-violet. Moreover, I grouped the achromatic colors, which range from white to grey to black.

6 CATEGORIZING FOOD BY COLOR 119

is the dominant color, US milk packing color schemes combine red + yellow, green + yellow, and blue + yellow, in contrast with Japanese color schemes.

It is widely recognized among US residents that specific color codes for milk cartons and their plastic lids are used by most manufacturers and retailers.[8] The following color categorization rules are not absolute, but are relatively widely established in the US:

- Whole milk = red
- Low-fat milk (1% and 2% are two common types) = dark blue or green
- Non-fat milk = blue, sometimes yellow

Even if consumers cannot read the words, they can quickly identify the milk fat content by looking at the color of the package or lid. For example, for its private-label organic milk, ShopRite,[9] a supermarket on the US East Coast, uses red packaging for whole milk, dark blue for 2%, green for 1%, and blue for non-fat milk. Other manufacturers vary in brightness and saturation, but most of their products have this color scheme.

As of 2023, there were no such color codes for milk cartons in Japan. For example, one dairy manufacturer's labels used green for whole milk, dark blue for low-fat, and red for fat-free, while another used dark blue for whole milk, green for low-fat, and blue for fat-free.[10] Why are the coloring conventions for milk cartons in the United States so different from those in Japan? The fact is that the United States was founded by immigrants, and the country places a high value on easily comprehensible information. In Japan, the milk fat content can be accurately determined by reading the text on the milk carton rather than relying on color.

In the case of Japanese dairy manufacturers, the colorimetric analysis of the images printed on the milk containers identified blues and greens of idyllic blue skies and grassy pasture landscapes. These images and colorimetric analysis results supported those of Hayakawa et al. that "most

[8] https://www.rd.com/article/milk-label-colors/.

[9] ShopRite (formerly Shop-Rite; founded 1946) is a supermarket retail cooperative with 321 stores on the East Coast across the six stores of Connecticut, Delaware, Maryland, New Jersey, New York, and Pennsylvania.

[10] Hidaka, K. (2015). A Comparative Cultural Study of Milk Carton Color Schemes and Designs in the U.S. and Japan. *Tama Art University Bulletin*, (30), pp. 155–163.

120   K. HIDAKA

(Japanese) milk cartons are white, blue, red, and green (yellow-green)."
In addition, Haruyo Ohno, an expert on the color environment in the
Color Science Association of Japan, pointed out that "Japanese packages and cartons are mostly achromatic (white, gray, black) + chromatic
color schemes," whereas "American color schemes are mostly chromatic
+ chromatic, making them look colorful."[11] In other words, it is possible
that Americans have become accustomed to vibrant color combinations
from a young age.

6.2   Package 2: American and Japanese Confectionery

Confectionery is a product we will likely encounter as often as milk from
childhood. In the US and Europe, Japanese confectionery is sold only
in Japanese grocery stores rather than in local supermarkets or department stores. Every year, Japanese confectionery companies introduce
fresh products to their customers, featuring seasonal and regional delicacies. What characteristics can be seen in the color schemes of these unique
confectionery packages? Between 2013 and 2014, I purchased 120 pieces
of confectionery (20 pieces each of the three categories: candies, chocolates, and gum) sold nationally in Japan and the United States. I used
colorimetry software to analyze the colors of the different candies' packages. Figure 6.5 shows the differences in the colors of confectionery
packages purchased in Japan and the United States. The color packaging of candy in Japan has more complex determinants than that of milk
cartons.

I purchased Japanese candy from convenience stores (Lawson Store
100), supermarkets (Aeon), and confectionery stores (Okashi no
Machioka) in Tokyo and Kanagawa Prefecture between June 2013 and
February 2014. I purchased the US candy from Wegman's and ACME
supermarkets in Cherry Hill, New Jersey, and from the Hudson News
convenience store stand at John F. Kennedy International Airport, New

---

[11] Presented in a poster on May 20, 2015, at Ochanomizu Sola City, Japan. Hidaka,
K. (2015, May 20). *A Comparison of Color Schemes and Images in the Package Design of
Sweets in the US and Japan*. Presented at AIC Tokyo 2015.

York, in May 2013 and April 2014. To account for differences in display and lighting, I also photographed the display shelves of the supermarkets and convenience stores where I purchased the candies (Figs. 6.3 and 6.4). These packages were digitally imaged,[12] and the five most representative colors of the 20 confections were extracted.[13] These are displayed in order in Fig. 6.5; the left column is for Japan, the right column is for the United States, and the color charts are for candy, chocolate, and gum from top to bottom.

Fig. 6.3 A candy store in Tokyo (2013)

---

[12] Colors were measured with X-rite's Color Munki and made into a color chart with a total of 100 color panels. Color Munki is a colorimeter and software package for color management from X-rite and Pantone.

[13] Hidaka, K. (2015). A Comparative Cultural Study of Milk Carton Color Schemes and Designs in the U.S. and Japan. *Tama Art University Bulletin*, (30), pp. 155–163.

122 K. HIDAKA

Fig. 6.4 The confectionery section in a supermarket in New Jersey, US (2013)

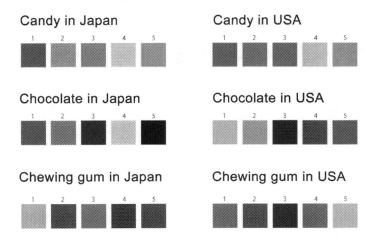

Fig. 6.5 Top 1–5 typical colors used in confectionery packaging

6.2.1 Candy

The use of red to yellow warm colors and gray is prevalent in Japanese candy packaging. The grayish colors look bright, soft, and dull. There is little use of green to purple. Overall, colors of medium brightness and medium vividness are standard. In addition, many Japanese candy packages include images of the candy's intended flavors (e.g., fruits and herbs) to evoke their taste via their colors.

US candy packaging has much in common with Japanese in the application of warm colors, albeit with two significant differences. First, the use of green is very common, and second, it should be noted that gray is not used at all. This tendency to use no gray resulted in vibrant, colorful packaging for US candy with low brightness and high saturation. These results were the same as those for the milk containers, where most of the colors on milk cartons in Japan are achromatic plus chromatic. At the same time, those in the United States are chromatic plus chromatic, making them look gaudy. Additionally, US candy packaging tends to present images of the candy inside the package, featuring dark and synthetic colors such as those used for condensed fruit juices and creams. In Japan, however, candy packaging emphasizes visual representation of the flavors the candies are supposed to offer.

6.2.2 Chocolate

I observed the most significant discrepancies in hue between Japan and the United States in the packaging of chocolate. In the case of Japanese chocolate, the most common hues for packaging are red, brown, black, and gold; owing to the influence of the products of major manufacturers, consumers associate the color black with bitterness and associate red with sweetness. Furthermore, the color of chocolate itself, brown mixed with red and black, is often used.

Concerning red candy packaging to remind consumers of the sweetness of milk chocolate, standard products such as Glico's Pocky and Lotte's Ghana Milk Chocolate[14] are packaged in red, and Lotte's derives from the red color of Swiss chocolate. At the beginning 1964, a Swiss engineer who was invited to establish the taste coined the catchphrase "Taste

---

[14] Nikkei Design (Ed.). (2012). *Textbook of Package Design*, pp. 184–189.

124   K. HIDAKA

of Switzerland"[15]; the packaging depicted a young girl in Swiss national dress, but the color was changed to red to evoke the Swiss flag. As the Ghana chocolate series became more cocoa-flavored and bitter, the theme color changed to black, and the white chocolate used cream-colored packaging.[16]

Meiji Company's milk chocolate packaging was initially influenced by that of the US Hershey's chocolate bars, with the dark brown and gold colors remaining virtually unchanged since its launch in 1926, except for 1940–1942 and 1951–1955. The packaging from 1955 to 2009 was the work[17] of Yusaku Kamekura, the designer who created the poster for the 1964 Tokyo Olympics. The current packages are also modernized versions of Kamekura's work by Landor Associates, with the same hues.

Even though many Japanese chocolate products are in the low price range, their packaging uses coated paper and the traditional sense of luxury in color scheme and texture. The fact that chocolate was a luxury item in Japan at the beginning of the twentieth century could still be influential today; even very inexpensive confections such as Tyrol[18] Chocolate and Black Thunder are particular about their packaging design. Tyrol designs its chocolate packaging to match flavors to holidays and seasons, such as New Year, Halloween, and Christmas, plus using characters such as Hello Kitty.

In contrast, American chocolate uses colors rarely used in Japanese chocolate, such as yellow and blue. Traditional American snack chocolates that are not chocolate bars, such as Milky Way and Reese's, also use orange and green, hues not found in Japanese chocolate. The most frequent hues in American packaging are brown, low-light gray, yellowish green, and blue. Hershey's[19] chocolate, which influenced Meiji Seika, is brown with silver-gray text. Some higher-priced chocolates have a sophisticated, upscale look even in the United States. M&Ms, introduced by Mars Candy Co. during World War II and inspired by the English eating

---

[15] Nikkei Design (Ed.). (2012). *Textbook of Package Design*, pp. 185–188.

[16] https://www.lotte.co.jp/kengaku/choco/history/ghana.html (Accessed: March 4, 2021).

[17] Kamekura, Y., et al. (Eds). (2005). *Yusaku Kamekura's Design.*

[18] Tyrol chocolate gets its name from the Tyrol region of Austria, similar to how Lotte's Ghana chocolate is derived from the cacao production area.

[19] The Hershey Company is one of the oldest and largest chocolate confectionery companies in the United States.

sugar-coated chocolates during the Spanish Civil War, were later sold to the US Army during World War II in the South Pacific; they were developed as a chocolate that could be eaten without melting, and they were later used in space food.[20] Today, chocolate is a cheap and readily available snack in Japan and the United States. However, in Japan, the packaging retains an air of foreign-derived luxury, while in the United States, it seems to have evolved into a colorful snack for soldiers.

6.2.3   Gum

In both Japan and the United States, the hues of gum packages are often yellow-green to blue-purple and silver (gray). These hues are thought to express strong cool menthol flavors. Conversely, gum packaging in both countries only infrequently uses orange and brown. The most frequent hue in Japanese gum packaging is silver (gray); Japanese gum packaging has a modern, inorganic feel with few hues and metallic colors. Separately, one gum flavor unique to Japan is *ume* (plum), which has a red color reminiscent of ripe plums and is reflected in four of the colors on the Japanese gum color chart.

In contrast, American gum packages use warmer colors than those in Japan. The colors represent flavors not sold in Japan, such as cinnamon, watermelon, and fruit mixes. Incidentally, there is an English color name, bubblegum, that refers to pink. (see Figure 3.5 in 3.8. Do Basic Color Terms (BCTs) and Traditional Color Names Matter for Gender?) The fourth color of American chewing gum in Figure 6.5 was the iconic bubblegum pink.

6.2.4   Limited Period/Region

When considering the hues of Japanese product packaging, one should not forget the unique Japanese limited-time-only and limited-region products. The red, yellow, and gold color of limited-time-only beer cans with "autumn flavor" and autumn leaves, or the white and blue colors of Hokkaido's classic souvenir confection *Shiroi Koibito* come to mind. Japanese manufacturers produce, along with standard products,

---

[20] https://www.history.com/news/the-wartime-origins-of-the-mm (Accessed: March 4, 2021).

126   K. HIDAKA

limited-run, limited-availability products based on the time of year or region.

The novelty of limited-availability products has a powerful appeal. In Japan, the color schemes differ between long-selling standard products and seasonal or regionally limited products, with the limited products having more temporary color schemes. Product scarcity increases the desire to purchase, and limited color schemes help denote that scarcity. Throughout Japan, regionally limited confections are often found in souvenir shops.

Japanese people have always respected the changing seasons and how they are reflected in the different colors, shapes, and ways of being on the earth. Perhaps this sensitivity permeates the hues of Japan's limited-time and limited-region products, and therefore, people seek a sense of seasonality and materiality in their food. As with the Heian aristocrats' tradition of *kasane no shikome*, in which they used the colors of their kimonos and personal belongings to represent the changing seasons, Japanese people subconsciously seek a reflection of the seasons in confectionery.[21] A typical example of this tendency can be observed in the fact that the same Japanese confectionery made of red bean paste and mochi rice is differently called *botan (n) mochi* in spring, *yofune* in summer, *ohagi (hagi)* in fall, and *kitamado* in winter. The same can be seen in *wagashi*, fresh confections, and the confectionery packages that line supermarket shelves.

In contrast, US seasonal foods are arranged around holidays such as Easter, Halloween, and Christmas, and regional product customization is rare. The United States is a large country with far fewer regional products than Japan. I am familiar with New York cheesecake, named after a place. Confections are widely available, with few regional limitations.

6.2.5   Blue Food Coloring and Packaging

The widespread use of blue to green is characteristic of American confectionery packaging. Readers who have heard the theory that blue is an

---

[21] Itagaki, A., & Okuda, S. (2012). Research on color of wrapping paper in Japanese-style confection shop in Kyoto, p. 63.

appetite suppressant[22] might wonder why blue is used so frequently on food packages in the United States.

In the post-World War II era, American color consultant Faber Birren noted that blue-colored foods tend to decrease appetite.[23] Research on the relationship between appetite and blue had a specific influence on American food development, and it is possible that the creative staff of Japanese food manufacturers absorbed these impressions. This earlier research conclusion could have been the reason for the extensive use of red and other warm colors in Japanese food packaging I observed in this study. Moreover, the colorimetric analysis revealed that US food and food packaging, unlike Japanese packaging practices, widely use blue and fluorescent colors, which do not exist much in nature.[24] Ai Hisano, a business historian, provides very detailed social background on the industrialization of food production and the rapid development of artificial coloring in early 20th-century America.[25] During the 1920s–1930s, the United States experienced what could have been called a "chromatic revolution," given the extensive marketing of foods with large amounts of chemical colorings,[26] including blue.

Another reason for using blue food and packaging in the United States relates to differences in indoor store lighting between the two countries. With the spread of LEDs in recent years, in-store illumination in the United States is becoming as bright as in Japan. As we saw in Chapter 3, Sect. 3.3, Haefelin pointed out that Germans prefer relatively low-illumination environments. Most confectionery display areas in

---

[22] Schlintl, C., & Schienle, A. (2020). Effects of Coloring Food Images on the Propensity to Eat: A Placebo Approach with Color Suggestions. *Frontiers in Psychology*, 11, 589826.

[23] Okuda, H., et al. (2002). Correlation between the Image of Food Colors and the Taste Sense: The Case of Japanese Twenties. *Journal of Cookery Science of Japan, 35* (1), p. 3.

[24] Brilliant Blue FCF, also known as Blue No. 1, is a food coloring agent used in various countries such as Japan, Europe, and the United States. It has undergone toxicity tests by the Joint FAO/WHO Expert Committee on Food Additives (JECFA) and has been deemed non-carcinogenic. This means it is safe for consumption and commonly used in artificially colored foods.

[25] Hisano, A. (2019). *Visualizing Taste: How Business Changed the Look of What You Eat*. Harvard University Press, pp. 22–29.

[26] Until the nineteenth century, coloring food was expensive, but it can now be done inexpensively.

Japan are brightly lit with fluorescent lights. In such environments, high brightness, low saturation, and warm colors (red to yellow) look good on packages. In contrast, confectionery display areas in US supermarkets and drugstores are often lit with incandescent lights. The Purkinje phenomenon of blue appearing bright in dimly lit areas[27] could be why blue is so often used on US confectionery packages, even with its high saturation and slightly lower brightness.

The colors of American cakes, which surprised me at the age of 16, resulted from an accumulation of lighting environments and taste preferences that were different from those where I grew up. However, I gradually became more accustomed to those colors and tastes as I became accustomed to seeing ambient light and eating those foods in my daily life. International exchange, ongoing research, and new theories suggest that the colors of Japanese and American packages may continue to change in the future. Foods come in various colors according to country, custom, plant and animal species, added coloring, food culture, and packages representing this variety of colors. I believe humans build up a diverse sense of color through daily observations of these representations.

6.3   LATER STORIES

In February 2019, a high school student from Saitama assigned fieldwork in the Tokyo metropolitan area came to my laboratory to ask me about the differences in food color perceptions between the United States and Japan. We discussed a subject that this high school student had posed: Why do the colors of food and packaging seem more vivid in the United States? This student had found my past papers online and thought discussing them would help the fieldwork.

As we saw in the Introduction, colors in the United States are often bright and vivid. This student hypothesized that because the United States is a multiracial nation, people use flashy colors to vehemently assert their individuality and make their presence easier to recognize. I told the student I thought it was possible but did not know. Indeed, food and food packaging color schemes express a national group tendency that transcends personal taste and the "character" of a particular country's products. Researchers have examined group tendencies regarding preferred

---

[27] Friedman, B. (1931). The Blue Arcs of the Retina. *Arch Ophthalmol*, 6(5), pp. 663–674.

6 CATEGORIZING FOOD BY COLOR   129

colors,[28] and surveys of milk containers and confectionery packaging are also part of this process. However, it would be extremely valuable if we could identify the reasons for these national tendencies through experimental research.

6.4   FOOD GROUPS COLORS

In a university co-op cafeteria in Tokyo, one day I noticed cryptic numbers on the receipt: "red 2.2, green 0.3, yellow 6.3" (Fig. 6.6). In Japan, as many people are aware, nutrition education is based on the "three-color good eating pattern," in which protein is classified as red for flesh and blood, carbohydrates as yellow for energy, and vegetables as green for body conditioning, and these are to be eaten in good balance. This three-color categorization began around the 1990s under the Association for the Promotion of Nutritional Improvement, which advocated balancing red, yellow, and green.[29] Some textbooks for lower and middle grades of elementary school use coloring books to teach the categorization of the three groups; Japanese students now appear to learn the three-color food categorization system from an early age, but I am from a different generation and was unaware of these color categorizations (adults in their thirties in Japan say it has been written on the school lunch menu since elementary school, whereas individuals in their forties and older learn about the system from their university cafeteria receipts). There is scope for research to determine whether this three-group dietary education is also provided in other countries.

The American food color-coding poster could serve as the origin of Japanese food color-coding education. Figure 6.7 is a poster from the War Food Administration during World War II, featuring a color wheel with seven food categories.[30] The illustration emphasizes the importance of healthy eating for preserving immunity, strong teeth, and overall well-being. The green group 1 includes green and yellow vegetables; the orange group 2 includes oranges and tomatoes; the blue group 3 includes

---

[28] Madden, T. J., Hewett, K., & Roth, M. S. (2000). Managing Images in Different Cultures: A Cross-National Study of Color Meanings and Preferences. *Journal of International Marketing*, 8(4), pp. 90–107.

[29] Nutrition Improvement Promotion Association (Ed.). (1990). *We Love Rice Food.*

[30] United States. War Food Administration. (1943). *Eat the Basic 7 ... EVERY day! Eat a Lunch that Packs a Punch!.* University of Minnesota Libraries.

Fig. 6.6 Receipt from the University of Tokyo Co-op Central Cafeteria marking three color food groups: red 2.2, green 0.3, and yellow 6.3 (2016)

potatoes and fruits; the white group 4 includes dairy products; the red group 5 includes meat, fish, and nuts; the brown group 6 includes bread and cereal; and the yellow group 7 includes butter and vitamin A. The poster encourages individuals to incorporate these foods into their diet for optimal health.

It is not only Japanese and American dietary education that classifies food by color. Mongolian cuisine is color-coded in its foods: Meat is called "red food" (улаан идээ), and dairy is called "white food" (цагаан идээ), perhaps based on the appearance of the two foodstuffs.[31] The same is true in Japan because meat (protein) is red. Still, dairy is classified differently in

---

[31] Arihara, K. (2014). 'White Food' and 'Red Food' in Mongolia. Bulletin of the Tohoku Animal Science and Technology Society, 64(1), pp. 1–6.

6 CATEGORIZING FOOD BY COLOR   131

Fig. 6.7 "*Eat the basic 7 ...: every day! eat a lunch that packs a punch*" by the War Food Administration (1943) (*Source* US Government Printing Office. University of Minnesota Libraries, Upper Midwest Literary Archives)

Japan, where dairy products fall into the red, yellow, and green categories because foods are classified according to how often they are consumed daily.

CHAPTER 7

Categorizing Identities by Color

The Gray soldiers prowl the cities ensuring order, ensuring obedience to the hierarchy. The Whites arbitrate their justice and push their philosophy. Pinks pleasure and serve in high color homes. Silvers count and manipulate currency and logistics. Yellows study the medicines and sciences. Greens develop technology. Blues navigate the stars. Coppers run the bureaucracy.

Every Color has a purpose.

Every color props up the Golds.
Pierce Brown, *Red Rising*.[1]

Pierce Brown's (1988–) *Red Rising* trilogy portrays a future dystopia, 700 years from the present day, where humankind has established colonies on other planets. The series made *The New York Times* bestseller list. The story is about the Reds, a terrorist group of people from the lowest caste who fight against the oppressive power exercised over the "lower colors" (the highest caste is gold), and the characters in the film made from the trilogy wear costumes and body colors that match their caste; they are also divided into different residential areas. Brown's writing was inspired by the plight of Irish immigrants in 19th-century

---

[1] Brown, P. (2014). *Red Rising*. Del Rey Books.

© The Author(s), under exclusive license to Springer Nature Switzerland AG 2024
K. Hidaka, *The Art of Color Categorization*,
https://doi.org/10.1007/978-3-031-47690-7_7

America,[2] working-class disenfranchisement, Greek tragedy, and Orwell's novel *1984*.[3] For instance, the red of the lowest class suggests the red hair of Irish immigrants. Brown has always attempted to portray the battles of social stratification through his stories. Although *Red Rising* is a fictional metaphor for a class struggle based on race and other factors, what is the history of dividing social status by color in real life?

7.1 CRESTS

The Bodi people (see Chapter 5) had colors, patterns, animals, and plants that they called morales as their symbols. These people conceptualized colors and patterns as birthstones, birth flowers, and the horoscope. Clear cultural indications of one's affiliation, character, and status through symbols, logos, and colors can be seen in the heraldry of many countries worldwide and have been observed since ancient times. Here, I look at the use of color to separate individuals, affiliations, armies, and organizations.

In medieval Europe, heraldry (referring to the regulation of coats of arms) originated in warfare and was used by diplomats in medieval wars and jousts. Initially, heralds (messengers who declared war) painted common symbols on shields, banners, and personal effects on their armor so they could be identified if they were killed in battle; in particular, the corpses of royalty, nobility and high-ranking officials were often brought back for funeral rites. These personal identifications gradually evolved into color coding to distinguish between friendly and enemy forces on the battlefield. Because these marks were used to distinguish friend and foe in battle, the color scheme had to be clear and visible even from a distance. This was further extended to marks indicating universities and organizations.[4]

Despite the seemingly colorful image of the coat of arms, only eight colors are commonly available, which is surprisingly few; orange and fur patterns are rarely used. This is because Western heraldry established rules for the use of colors to ensure visibility. The only colors that can be used are the metal of gold and silver; red, blue, orange, green, purple, and

---

[2] https://www.nytimes.com/2018/01/26/books/review/pierce-brown-red-rising-best-seller.html (Accessed: March 4, 2021).

[3] https://www.youtube.com/watch?v=6S17Kc8lDgs (ABS-CBN News).

[4] Mori, M. (2022). *An Introduction to Heraldry*. Chikuma Shobo.

7 CATEGORIZING IDENTITIES BY COLOR **135**

black colors; and the fur pattern. Coats of arms showing gold and silver were given exceptionally high value. Here, I take a closer look at the rules of color use (Fig. 7.1). The color of the coat of arms is called the tincture, and the three categories are (1) metals, (2) colors, and (3) furs.

(1) metals—gold (*or*) and silver (*argent*): In painting colors, gold was substituted for yellow and silver for white.
(2) colors—red (*gules*), blue (*azure*), black (*sable*), green (*vert*), purple (*purpure*), deep red (*sanguine*), and only rarely orange (*tenny*). No intermediate or pastel colors were allowed.
(3) fur—furs were "ermine," "vair," and "potent," but they were used infrequently.

The rules for coats of arms were that they should have two colors, one for the ground and one for the pattern, and that gradations and the like were in violation. This is a reasonable rule for visual clarity. In addition, when combining two colors from categories (1) through (3), metal on metal (e.g., yellow on white), color on color (e.g., green on red), fur on fur, and gray and pastel colors were all prohibited. Gray and pastel colors are difficult to distinguish from a distance; white/yellow combinations are hard to see. Combinations of opposite colors like vivid red and green are prone to border halos, and patterns look cluttered. I assume that these rules of thumb, which were difficult to understand in actual competition, led to the establishment of these prohibitions.

An interesting point to consider is the unique origin and characteristics of Japan's family crests, *Kamon,* compared to their European counterparts. Unlike European crests, primarily used for personal identification in times of war, Japanese crests were designed as symbols for families. One notable distinction is that Japanese crests are monochromatic. Family crests spread from the staining of banner seals on the oxcarts of court nobles during the Heian period, around the eleventh to twelfth centuries, roughly the same time as in Europe. A white circle was dyed out of the crest, and then a painter would draw a design on top of the crest within the circle. As a result, many of the coats of arms have symmetrical patterns that fit within the circular shape. These were all marks to identify "my cart" with a cloth flag on an oxcart that looked almost the same. However, during the Warring States period (1467–1615), these Japanese

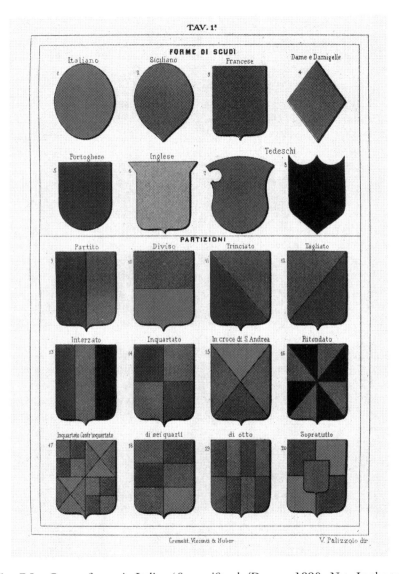

Fig. 7.1 Coats of arms in Italian (*Source* iStock/Duncan 1890; *Note* In the top row of the eight one-color coats of arms, from left to right, are the ovals representing the Italian, Sicilian, French, and female coats of arms. The Portuguese, English, and two German styles are in the lower row. The bottom half, 12 types, are the various divided designs of the coat of arms)

7 CATEGORIZING IDENTITIES BY COLOR   137

crests were changed to use as flag marks to indicate the army to which they belonged, just as in Europe.[5]

7.2   Collar Insignia of the Japanese Military

Just as European heraldry developed out of battle, the increasing number of colors to be identified by flags, coats of arms, etc., is attributed to war. In the former Japanese army, officially founded in 1871, the colors of arms (*Waffenfarbe* in German) identified the type of soldiers. The different levels of German soldiers wore collar badges of different colors to distinguish them. For instance, in the case of the army, shrimp brown was the engineers, yellow was the artillery, black was the military police, indigo was the Transportation Corps,[6] and red was the infantry.[7]

This color scheme was probably intended to convey to Japanese children what the military was like before the war. In *Norakuro*,[8] a popular manga by Suiho Tagawa that was serialized in magazines during the prewar and wartime Showa periods in Japan, a double-page spread is devoted to color coding the different types of soldiers (Fig. 7.2). *Norakuro* is a manga cartoon that depicts the military in a heartwarming atmosphere, without any cruel scenes. Still, it does depict the mechanisms that existed in the Japanese military in some places. In Fig. 7.2 the military police are described as black, infantry as red, cavalry as green, artillery as yellow, engineers as a steeplejack, airmen as light blue, transportation as indigo, accountants as silver brown, medical personnel as dark green, veterinarians as purple, and military musicians as dark blue. The colors of these military uniforms are almost identical to those in *The Pictorial Book of Japanese Military Uniforms*. However, some color names are not so familiar to us today.

---

[5] https://www.gov-online.go.jp/eng/publicity/book/hlj/html/202212/202212_03_en.html (Accessed: August 9, 2023).

[6] A branch of the Imperial Japanese Army that oversaw logistics (munitions) supply.

[7] Hirayama, S. (2018). *The Pictorial Book of Japanese Military Uniforms: Meiji Period*. Kokushokan, pp. 602–603.

[8] Tagawa, S. (1969). *Norakuro Platoon Commander*. S. Tagawa©, 1936. Norakuro is an anthropomorphic black and white dog inspired by Felix the Cat.

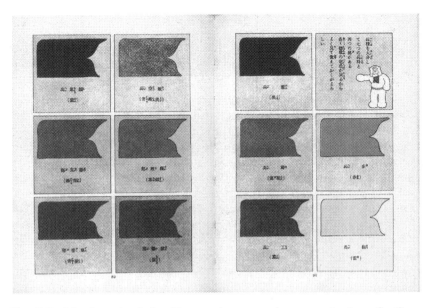

Fig. 7.2 Norakuro by Suiho Tagawa showcases the categorization of military collar insignia based on color (1936)

In the former Japanese army and navy, the ranks of soldiers were distinguished by the number of stars and lines on their shoulder patches. Even today, the military forces of many countries still use colors, marks, and lines to distinguish rank, and I next examine this use of colors and patterns.

7.3 Ranks

Yellow has been the color of the Emperor in China since ancient times. It is even known as the forbidden color because of the golden yellow robe which only Chinese emperors are allowed to wear. This color was chosen because of its prominence. Although purple is not included in the Chinese five primary colors of red, yellow, blue, white, and black, it is still the second most respected color. It was considered sacred as the color of the gods and the immortals, and sometimes the color of the emperor. Additionally, dark colors with high saturation were the most respected in

Chinese clothing, while light colors were considered suitable for lower ranks.

In Japan, colors for class identification of Chinese origin were determined around the Asuka period (592–710 CE). The Twelve Grades of Crown Rank, established by Prince Shotoku in 603, is well known among most Japanese. The coronation was modeled after Confucianism, in which the 12 ranks were divided into large and small levels of virtue, benevolence, propriety, faith, righteousness, and wisdom. Six colors were designated for the crowns and robes of court subjects, purple, blue, red, yellow, white, and black, and lightness of shade distinguished higher (darker) from lower (lighter) ranks. This customary system of the imperial court, court nobles, and warrior families is called *yushoku kojitsu*.[9] In Japan, bureaucrats were ranked by color under the Twelve Grades of Crown Rank system. The Chinese Sui dynasty's politics influenced this Japanese system. The colors used were purple, blue, red, yellow, white, and black. It was strictly prohibited to wear a color higher than one's rank.

The number and types of color rankings for imperial court costumes have evolved over time. A literature survey by Yukichika Maeda revealed difficulties distinguishing purple from scarlet; he explained that the initial classification of eight colors was reduced to six and eventually to four.[10] According to Maeda, this color-coded ranking also has a practical medical benefit. In 647 CE, a law was passed to rank the colors dyed with medicinal herbs and to determine rank according to the color of the imperial court uniform. Because there was no proper bathing custom in ancient times, people are said to have dyed cloth using dyes with medicinal properties as a preventive against skin diseases and insects.[11] The red color dyed with madder and the brown cloth dyed with chestnut did not merely establish class and hierarchy but also meant medical prophylaxis.

Ancient Japan had its standards for color properties that indicated high rank. In dyeing and weaving, the actual colors that could be produced varied according to the skill level and difficulty of obtaining the materials.

---

[9] Hachijo, T. (2020). *Illustrated Guide to the Colors of Yushoku: Japanese Traditional Colors*. Tankōsha, pp. 190–191.

[10] Maeda, Y. (1960). *A History of Japanese Color Culture*, "Invasion of Purple and Scarlet," p. 301.

[11] Maeda, U. (1980). *Color: Dye and Color (Mono to Ningen no Bunka Shi 38)*. Hosei University Press, pp. 201–213.

140   K. HIDAKA

The pinnacle of the forbidden/permitted color of ceremonial dress for the emperor's accession is reddish-brown *kohrozen*. According to Yukio Yoshioka, an expert on the history of dyeing and weaving, *kohrozen* is a forbidden color for which the dyeing process is complicated, and it is difficult to produce the same color consistently. *Kohrozen* has an iridescent mystique that changes significantly in appearance under sunlight and artificial lighting.[12]

People highly regarded materials that possessed structural color. Structural color is a phenomenon in which light is reflected and scattered by the material's structure, without chemical dyes, making it appear iridescent. The wings of morpho butterflies are famous for displaying this property. Fabrics that changed color depending on the illumination, in a phenomenon known as metamerism, were highly valued. As we saw in Chapter 5 with the categorization of the colors *hare* and *ke*, the Japanese considered that the exquisiteness of the materials used, how long they took to produce, or the bewitching appearance of iridescent colors, depending on the angle and lighting, reflected high class.

The prohibition of certain colors was relaxed in the aristocratic culture of the Heian period (794–1185 CE), which ushered in a golden age of color and gave birth to many elegant color names. The world's oldest color scheme handbook, *Kasane no irome*, was used by the aristocracy at court during the Heian period and applied to everything from costumes to furnishings. There were several types of *kasane*:

- Inner and outer kimono fabrics in two colors for a layered color scheme.
- Layering kimonos of different colors (*juni-hitoe*).
- Weaving different color threads between the warp and weft yarns to create an iridescent effect.

Each color scheme was given an elegant Japanese name, and the seasons in which it could be used and the ages at which it could be worn were specified. The color schemes were closely linked to the colors of nature, plants, and animals in each of the four seasons, and even the subtle changes in color with the changing of the seasons were unfailingly incorporated. As a result, the number of color schemes reached more than 200. While

[12] Yoshioka, Y. (2000). *A Dictionary of Japanese Colors.*

some color schemes could be used throughout the four seasons, taste and education were reflected in how nobles arranged their costumes with colors that suited the season.

This culture was influenced by the tradition of incorporating into designs the external environment of Japan, located in a temperate zone with widely changing seasons, and by introducing customs such as the 24 solar terms imported from China, which divided the calendar in detail. The calendar, which divides the year into four seasons (spring, summer, autumn, and winter) and the ceremonies of weddings, funerals, and other occasions, tended to make the color scheme rules more detailed than usual.

7.4 SUMPTUARY LAWS

The concept of class ranking by color has been demonstrated before, but the ancient Celts took it to another level with particularly tight color control. They lived in a vast region spanning from central to Western Europe, including the islands of Britain and Ireland. Social class was distinguished by colors, based on the Irish Code of Ethics of the seventh and eighth centuries. According to the law, yellow and black were for the ruled; gray, brown, and red were for the nobility of the ruling class; and purple and blue were for royalty. Slaves were allowed to wear only one color, the ruled people were limited to two colors, the intelligentsia to six colors, and the ruling class seven colors.[13] To wear colorful clothing, one had to be of a higher social class.

Many cultures in the world have long enforced laws related to class, such as sumptuary laws that prohibited owning luxuries, and these laws outline precisely what is or is not legal.[14] Colors, too, can be regulated or encouraged by law, resulting in unique uses. For instance, to circumvent the loophole in the law banning luxuries, the Japanese language has a history of deliberately mangling color categorizations so that color names are inaccurate.

[13] Nicolle, D. (1984). *Arthur and the Anglo-Saxon War*. Osprey Publishing, p. 21.

[14] Morozumi, Y. (2001). Categorization in Islamic Law, University of Tokyo Sogo Kenkyukai (Ed.). (2001). *Dividing (Wakeru, University of Tokyo Open Lecture 73)*. p. 81.

142   K. HIDAKA

During Japan's Edo period (1603–1867 CE), many color names were produced that did not match their hue. In the Bunka-Bunsei era (1804–1829 CE), when Edo-machi culture was thriving, a large number of customary color names based on brown (tea) and rat (gray) were created. They were so numerous that they became known as *shijuhachi cha hyaku nezumi* "The Forty-eight Tea and A Hundred Rats." These color names were derived from the names of people and places, making it difficult to visualize their hue.

In the Edo period, four social classes, known as *shi-noh-ko-sho* (The four occupations), existed: samurai, peasants, artisans, and merchants, Various restrictions were imposed on everything from dress to diet so that status could be immediately apparent. The shogunate enforced the thrift ordinance, prohibiting extravagance among the ordinary people, such as wearing luxurious fabrics dyed in purple or madder; people belonging to lower castes were restricted to wearing only brown (tea), gray (rat), and indigo in their garments. However, some among the merchant class were substantially better off than the samurai; as a way of escape, these merchants deceptively called red or purple cloth brown or rat colors. Interestingly, these names were also used to describe shades of pink, green, and purple, which helped people evade sumptuary laws. In another example of evading sumptuary laws, the color name *Saga Nezumi* was a dark smoky pink, the same name as an elegant area in Kyoto. In addition to place names like *Saga* in Kyoto, *kabuki* actor names, and tea master names, such as *Rikyu Nezumi* (Rikyu Rat), are added at the end of the word "tea/rat." These merchants gave names justifying the brown/rat color of their kimonos to avoid breaking the law. The hues of colors bearing the names of *kabuki* actors or tea masters did not look brown/gray. The result of suppression and the superficial appearance of adhering to regulations was the mass production of tea and rat color names. These color names were considered facetious ways of defying the law.

This color naming: the Forty-eight Tea and A Hundred Rats was a popular trend in Edo fashion, featuring brown and gray tones and giving rise to cryptic color names. This reflects the mystique of Japanese culture and the creativity of Japanese people striving to wear any color of their choice.

7 CATEGORIZING IDENTITIES BY COLOR   143

Tatemae is a term used to describe the public moral standards that are a significant aspect of Japanese culture.[15] Even if the colors of true intention (*honne*) and *tatemae* are different, the majority of Japanese people might not feel (or be paralyzed by) the fear of being sanctioned for going against social norms. It is a mystery as to whether the Forty-eight Tea and A Hundred Rats of the Edo period, in which visible colors and color names were contradictory, were connected to a psychological mechanism in which blue and green are recognized as different hues. People commonly refer to "blue lights" and "blue apples" without being aware of any contradiction in their use. This could be related to the fact that the people of Japan follow the opinions of their superiors and neighbors, saying that it is customary or the law, even if the names are different from the color discrimination that they can see.

Language and dialects are means of communication that are largely democratic and shaped by the tonal pressure of how the majority speaks. In other words, the path of most language development is that the language of the majority becomes the standard language.[16] Although language is a means of mutual communication, the demand to speak the same language as those around you can impose a kind of pressure. Pressure to conform is the pressure on a person with a minority opinion to implicitly conform to the majority opinion when making decisions within a particular group. Even if the color you see is inconsistent with your original color name understanding, if you are exposed to cultural, linguistic, or legal pressures for long enough, you will not be aware of it because "that's just the way it is."

In 21st-century Japan, hair color expression is a subject of syncretism. During the peak job-hunting season, it is common to see university students re-dyeing their hair from its previous green, pink, or gold back to black for job interviews. They also wear black suits that they would not normally wear. They believe conforming to the majority public opinion is safer, and that companies are more likely to accept them that way rather than if they express themselves through their preferred hair color.

[15] Naito, T., & Gielen, U. P. (1992). *Tatemae* and *Honne*: A Study of Moral Relativism in Japanese Culture. *Psychology in International Perspective*, 50, pp. 161–172.

[16] The standard language used here refers to the indigenous naturally occurring language, not the official language enforced by law or other means in a colony or multilingual nation.

7.5 Landscape Laws

The terms harmony and decorum characterize the direction of color schemes. Harmony is of Greek origin and used in Japanese for color,[17] music, and taste; decorum is of Latin origin and is a rhetorical term meaning "propriety."[18] Decor means beauty, appearance, elegance, charm, or ornamentation (cf. Art Deco). From the landscape design perspective, the installation of buildings and signs that destroy the atmosphere of a cityscape is contrary to this ethic of harmony and decorum.

Regulations on color and design, mainly for buildings, advertisements, billboards, and outdoor installations, have long existed in Europe and the United States. The Landscape Law, which legislates the very same harmony and decorum, is a law that has been enforced by local governments in Japan since 2004.[19] Local government landscape guidelines include approved Munsell values and color charts that indicate the allowable hue, lightness, and saturation for use in buildings, signs, and installations under the law. The guidelines which new buildings and outdoor commercial signs must follow aim for harmony between architecture, building decorations and installations, and materials unique to the local area. For instance, many villages in the Cotswolds in England, described by William Morris (1834–1896), a proponent of the Arts and Crafts Movement, as among the most beautiful in England, are lined with houses built of honey-colored Cotswold stone, a unique limestone found only in this region.

Ashiya City, Hyogo Prefecture, a municipality that enforces landscape guidelines that are among the strictest in Japan, also requires in its guidelines that buildings and outdoor advertisements be installed in harmony with the original landscape and the ground color of the land. In July 2009, Ashiya City decided to designate the entire city area as the Ashiya Landscape District under the Landscape Law. The city has officially designated the Ashiya River area as a special landscape area. Almost all the

---

[17] Moon, P., & Spencer, D. E. (1944). Aesthetic Measure Applied to Color Harmony. *JOSA*, 34(4), pp. 234–242.

[18] Hariman, R. (1992). Decorum, Power, and the Courtly Style. *Quarterly Journal of Speech*, 78(2), pp. 149–172.

[19] Utsumi, M., Kobayashi, S., & Sakai, F. (2006). A Study on the Institutional Transition from Landscape Ordinance to Landscape Law: A Case Study of Odawara City, Kanagawa Prefecture. *City Planning Review*, 41, pp. 319–324.

ground in the Hanshin area where Ashiya City is located is covered with granite, especially along the Ashiya River, where the stone walls of the riverbed and riverbanks and the stone walls of mansions that have stood since the late Meiji period are all made of granite. As with the Cotswolds in England, the colors produced by the materials unique to the area create the landscape, and it will continue to be important to match the colors of natural materials with those of manmade objects such as advertisements and architecture to maintain a harmonious landscape.

In 2015, a curious event occurred in Kyoto Prefecture, where the Landscape Law affected the classification of colors. Many municipalities in Kyoto Prefecture, like Ashiya City, have strict landscape guidelines. In one, Kyotanabe City, the city government asked Doshisha University's Kyotanabe Hall to change its exterior wall color to brown under the Landscape Law because the first proposal was gray. Sticking to the first proposal, the construction company insisted that the color was brown because the Munsell values measured by the machine were yellowish-red. *The Munsell Book of Color* defines brown as being in the "yellow–red family, with medium to low lightness and saturation in the low to mid-range."[20] Thus, persuaded by the construction company, Doshisha University allowed the construction as it was, even though the accurate saturation, 0.5, was so low that it did indicate gray. According to the Doshisha University students, the school built a hall that looks gray, but the university stated it was brown.[21]

As I have demonstrated in this chapter, the prohibition of certain colors, such as in the Edo period's sumptuary laws and the modern Landscape Law, gave rise to new names and definitions for colors. In the Edo period, there were no Munsell values or color measuring devices, so no matter what color was used, it was acceptable to call it brown or gray. Today, because of color measuring machines, it is possible to use the Munsell value for a color that looks gray but has a Munsell value in the yellowish-red range and claim that it is brown. In this age of color measurement, a new grayish color name, "Doshisha University Brown," may be established in the next few decades.

---

[20] Munsell Color Company. (1929). *Munsell Book of Color*. Baltimore, p. 28.

[21] *Yomiuri Shinbun.* (2015, July 31).

CHAPTER 8

Categorizing People by Color

I was born in a family full of color. Even if I appear black, I am also white and native Indian too.

Angélica Dass, "The beauty of human skin in every color" at TED 2016.[1]

In this chapter, I describe categories of people based on their physical color. Brazilian photographer Angélica Dass was born into a mixed-race family of black, white, and Native American descent. In her Humanae Project, created to represent the equality and beauty of different races, she displays people's skins against the backgrounds of thousands of portraits, giving them Pantone identification numbers. She continues to promote the diversity of human color on the internet and in exhibitions in different countries.

I would also like to describe an experience my nephew had when he was eight years old. His mother (my sister) is Japanese, born in Tokyo and living in the United States, and his father is European-American. My nephew, who is half-Japanese, has a strong European appearance. One day, while my nephew was with his mother, a European-American Caucasian man asked him: "Does your father look like you or your mother?".

---

[1] https://www.ted.com/talks/angelica_dass_the_beauty_of_human_skin_in_every_c olor. February 2016.

© The Author(s), under exclusive license to Springer Nature Switzerland AG 2024
K. Hidaka, *The Art of Color Categorization*,
https://doi.org/10.1007/978-3-031-47690-7_8

148   K. HIDAKA

It was a malicious question, but in essence, this man was interested in what race my nephew's father resembled because his Asian mother was obviously different from his European appearance. However, my nephew did not immediately understand the intention behind this question. He could not answer it: his parents were just "parents," and he had no experience categorizing them by skin color or race. By vocalizing new categorizations, such as "this person is white" or "he/she is yellow," my nephew was almost forced to recognize them as different races with different skin colors. In other words, my nephew learned from this white man that society differentiates people based on the color of their skin. Sadly, my sister told me, "I wanted my son to grow up with a pure heart all his life, so I didn't want him to be aware of the racism in this world." Drawing attention to racial differences at an early age can lead to discrimination as children begin to categorize people based on appearance.

According to the Belgian social anthropologist Barbara Saunders, humans sort new things they encounter based on their experiences, representing them with things they already know. For example, we process red as follows: (1) red object → (2) gives the experience of seeing red → (3) motivates the vocalization "this is red" → (this answer which also implies) "[this is not green or purple or any other color]."

Similarly, according to this mechanism of recognition and categorization, my nephew learned the following: (1) the faces of the European father and Asian mother and his own biracial face → (2) the experience of seeing them as different color races → (3) questions to vocalize "my father looks like my face" → (4) my mother is not white.

Humans distinguish between peers and nonpeers by categorizing the color of their bodies (skin, eyes, hair) and tend to be wary of those with different appearances. Further, even if it is only a distinction, there is a history of enforcing social profit-and-loss conditions based on body color, reflected in the construct of race.

8.1   RACES

In English, "color" means color and race, that is, colored people. In the Republic of South Africa, the apartheid policy of 1948–1994 separated races by skin color to normalize discrimination against the black race. *Apartheid* means "separation, segregation" in Afrikaans, and Nelson Mandela (1918–2013), a politician who would become the country's

8 CATEGORIZING PEOPLE BY COLOR   **149**

president in 1994, was imprisoned for 27 years for his resistance to apartheid policies. Mandela wrote the following words in his autobiography, published after he became president:

> *No one is born hating another person because of the color of his skin, or his background, or his religion. People must learn to hate, and if they can learn to hate, they can be taught to love, for love comes more naturally to the human heart than its opposite.*
> *The Long Walk to Freedom: The Autobiography of Nelson Mandela.*[2]

Just as my nephew never once considered categorizing his parents by skin color until a white person questioned him about it, categorizing and hating people by skin color is not innate; it is learned.

As I have repeatedly noted, there are similarities between Western color categorizations and the logic of racism. Western cultures have ranked white at the top of value hierarchies and black at the bottom, with an underlying assumption of a "pure color," an imaginary concept. The purpose of segregation was to prevent the mixing of colors, and eugenics guided laws prohibiting the mixing of blood between whites and people of color. Similarly, American grocery stores and supermarkets have the custom of identifying the contents of their products by the color of their labels, as seen in the example of color-coded fat content on packages and lids.

Eugenics, a system of beliefs aimed at improving human genetic quality, gained popularity in the nineteenth century with the advent of Darwin's theory of evolution. Eugenics incorporates the study of the various Darwinian categories of plants and animals and includes defining hierarchies and pure breeds. Eugenic thought had existed since ancient Greece, but eugenics was incorporated into politics and society as a science and practice inspired by Darwin.

For instance, the British sociologist Herbert Spencer (1820–1903) applied Darwin's concept of natural selection to human society and popularized the well-known idea of the survival of the fittest. From the late nineteenth century to the early twentieth century, attempts were made to provide academic support for eugenics to justify scientific racism and policies. Following the theories of biologists Hans Friedrich Karl

---

[2] Mandela, N. (1996). *The Long Road to Freedom: The Autobiography of Nelson Mandela.* Japanese translation by Agarie, K. NHK Publications.

Günther, Eugen Fischer, and other anthropologists, biologists, hygienists, economists, geographers, historians, and sociologists were mobilized[3] to categorize humans and assign a pecking order of superiority where the most important indicator of superiority or inferiority was race.

Johann Friedrich Blumenbach (1752–1840), the German comparative anatomist, zoologist, and anthropologist, is credited with the first definition of race. Considered the founder of anthropology, he divided the races into five categories in 1795: Caucasian (white), Mongolian (yellow), Ethiopian (black), American (red), and Malay (brown).[4] The terms Caucasoid and Mongoloid derive from this classification, which came to dominate anthropology and racial science. The categorization of "race," which became a hallmark of racial science, is based on the idea that humans are born with inherent genetic differences based on outward appearance.[5] Lévi-Strauss, who grew up in a Jewish family, defined ideas of racism as follows:

1. There are certain correlations between genetic and intellectual ability and moral disposition.
2. This genetic component, which correlates with intellectual ability and moral disposition, is valid for all members of a given human population.
3. Such human groups are called "races," and a hierarchical order of superiority and inferiority can be established among these races according to the quality of their genetic elements.
4. Based on their differences, the superior race can dominate, exploit, and sometimes eradicate the inferior race.[6]

The French aristocrat and writer Count Arthur de Gobineau, in his *An Essay on the Inequality of the Human Races* (1853), ranked humans into three races, writing that "The negroid variety is the lowest, and stands at the foot of the ladder..." The Yellow race is described as "the yellow man

---

[3] Burleigh, M., & Wippermann, W. (1991). *The Racial State: Germany 1933–1945*, pp. 51–73.

[4] Saini, A. (2019). *Superior: The Return of Race Science*. Fourth Estate, pp. 11–16. Blumenbach, J. F. (1795). *De generis humani varietate native*. Vandenhoek & Ruprecht.

[5] Saini, A. (2019). *Superior: The Return of Race Science*. Fourth Estate, pp. 11–16.

[6] Lévi-Strauss, C., & Eribon, D. (1991/2008). *Conversations With Claude Levi-Strauss* (Originally written in French, Takeuchi, Trans.). Misuzu shobo, pp. 268–269.

has little physical energy, and is inclined to apathy..." Then finally, the White people he belongs to "are gifted with reflective energy, or rather with an energetic intelligence."[7]

The definition of race also had a major ripple effect on Japan. Around the same time that the "rainbow is seven colors" categorization was introduced to Japan after the country opened to the outside world, Blumenbach's racial categorization and stereotypes were also introduced. At the end of the nineteenth century, a set of Japanese ideologies called "de-Asianization and Westernization" was supported by many scholars. Yukichi Fukuzawa (1834–1901), a political philosopher and educator, adopted British and German academics and technology during the Meiji era and advocated de-Asianization, but white supremacy was latent in his thought. In the "Race Theory" section of Fukuzawa's *Bankoku List* (1898), he classified the world's races into five races living on five continents—white, yellow, red, brown, and black—in other words, by skin color.[8] Based on modern European thought and eugenics of the late nineteenth century, this pamphlet popularized the concept of race. Blumenbach's strong influence can be easily seen in Fukuzawa's description of skin color categories:

1. Whites are "beautiful in appearance and highly civilized."
2. The yellow race "has skin as yellow as oil, narrow eyes, industrious, but not very advanced."
3. Reds, "with red and brown skin and rugged personalities, are the 'natives' of North and South America."
4. Blacks "have dark skin, frizzy hair, etc., and have never known civilized progress."
5. Brown people "whose skin is an austere shade of brown, fierce in character, and live on islands."[9]

While Fukuzawa himself belonged to the Asian race, he set aside his own racial identity, and his writings strongly promoted the idea of white

---

[7] Saini, A. (2019). *Superior: The Return of Race Science*. Fourth Estate, p. 58.

[8] Fukuzawa, Y. (1869). *Shochu bankoku ichiran (A Catalog of Nations in the Palm of Your Hand)*. Tokyo, pp. 5–94.

[9] Fukuzawa, Y. (1869). *Shochu bankoku ichiran (A Catalog of Nations in the Palm of Your Hand)*. Tokyo, pp. 5–94.

152   K. HIDAKA

(Caucasian) superiority. Influenced by cutting-edge European theories of evolution, he, who played a key role in introducing Western-style modernization during the Meiji era, simultaneously propagated ideas of racial superiority.

The biggest problem with eugenics-based policies is that they support the government and others in power in discriminating against and mistreating the vulnerable; an additional problem is that genetic and cultural diversity are lost because of artificial eugenics policies. The social, economic, political, and physical segregation based on the race hierarchy that was specifically called racial segregation began following the end of the Civil War in the form of what were known as the Jim Crow laws from 1876 to 1964 in the United States, of "White Australia" policies from 1890 until the mid-1970s, and of apartheid in South Africa until 1994.[10] Systemic racism is the institutionalization of practices that perpetuate generational disadvantages in life. It is closely associated with scientific racism, which involves using scientific measurements such as anthropometry (which examines skeletal structure, skin, hair, etc.) to categorize human races. Biologists employed similar methods in categorizing plants and animals based on their differences to create color charts for classifying humans according to their physical features.

Three aspects of the amount and proportion of pigment produced by the melanocytes in the iris determine eye color: the pigment of the epithelial cells, the melanin attached to the iris stroma, and the density of these cells. Incidentally, the irises of many Caucasian infants start bluish but gradually change to brown, hazel, amber, blue, green, gray, blue-violet, and so on. Color charts and color wheels for the human body were initially intended for medical and cosmetic use. For example, they were used to determine the condition of urine, eyes, hair, and skin by color, and as an indicator for dyeing hair. However, the Nazis measured whether a person was Aryan or not by whether they were blonde-haired and blue-eyed (Figs. 8.1 and 8.2).

Why did they do this? In the 1920s, Germany, which had lost World War I and had to pay substantial postwar reparations, was in chaos due to hyperinflation. Banknotes with astronomical values in the hundreds of millions of marks were issued daily, and prices continued to rise. Germany was also engulfed by the Great Depression, which began in 1929, and

[10] Wildman, S. M. (1996). *Privilege Revealed: How Invisible Preference Undermines America*. NYU Press, p. 87.

Fig. 8.1 Comparison of hair color of Aryan race during Nazi Germany (1937) (*Source* Fritz Carl [akg-images])

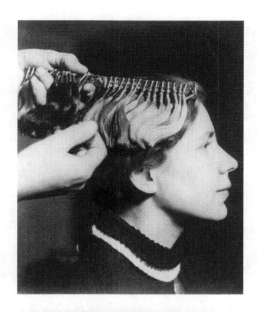

Fig. 8.2 Comparison of eye color of Aryan race during Nazi Germany (1937) (*Source* Fritz Carl [akg-images])

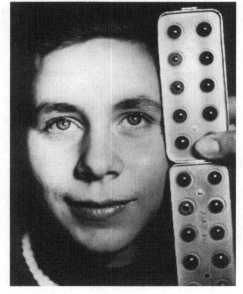

154 K. HIDAKA

the country was filled with starving, unemployed people. Adolf Hitler (1889–1945) increased public works projects and the police and military to create jobs and instigated the polemic that the depression was caused by foreigners taking Germans' jobs and that it was useless to keep alive those who could not work simply by spending taxpayers' money on them. Economic insecurity gave rise to Hitler's regime, which was converted into energy to exclude the handicapped, the weak, and foreigners. In *Mein Kampf*, a projection of his racial views from around 1925, Hitler wrote, "When the Aryan race interbred with the more inferior races, the result invariably stopped being the hand of culture."[11] Hitler strongly advocated Aryan (white) race superiority and the prohibition of mixed blood with people of color. The skin color chart (Fig. 8.3), created by anthropologist Felix von Luschan, a German Society for Racial Hygiene member, started with the number 1 white and ended with 36 black. On September 15, 1935, ten years after publication of *Mein Kampf*, the German government passed the Law for the Protection of German Blood and Honor and the Reich Citizenship Law, commonly known as the Nuremberg Laws, to maintain the "purity" of German blood.

Based on the Nuremberg Laws, the Nazi rulers classified German citizens according to appearance, religion, sexual preference, and disability. According to the Nazis, white people with blond hair and blue eyes were the superior Aryan race and were segregated from non-Aryan races. Unmarried women with blue eyes were sent to the *Lebensborn* (Fount of Life) to increase the population of the pure Aryan race. Heinrich Luitpold Himmler (1900–1945), a high-ranking commissioner in the Nazi SS, advocated for a policy in which Aryan German men were encouraged to engage in sexual relationships exclusively with women in the *Lebensborn*. He also enacted laws that criminalized interracial marriages.[12]

8.2 Yellow on Nazi Concentration Camp Badges

There is a very deep connection between color and the Nazis. Nazi Germany also set up camps of the opposite kind to *Lebensborn*, where non-Aryan races Germany classified as Jewish or Sinti-Roma (known as

---

[11] Hitler, A. (1973). *Mein Kampf* (I. Hirano & S. Shozumi, Trans.), p. 372.

[12] Whitman J. Q. (2017). Hitler's American Model: The United States and the Making of Nazi Race Law. (No. 1533/4267) [Kindle].

Fig. 8.3 Skin color chart, Berlin, Germany by Prof. Dr. Felix von Luschan (*Source* Peabody Museum of Archaeology and Ethnology at Harvard University. *Note* 6.6 × 9.3 × 1.4 cm. Skin color chart of 36 glass mosaic pieces set in the double-sided brass tray with numbers; tray in brass sleeve; marked Hautfarber-Tafel/2. Auflage nach/Prof. Dr. Felix von Luschan/Puhl and Wagner-G. Heinersdorff/Berlin-Treptow/Werkstatten für Mosaik und Glasmalerei)

gypsies) were sent to die: the concentration camps throughout Germany and Poland. In November 1939, the Nazis required all Jews in Poland to wear a yellow Star of David for identification (Fig. 8.4). This order was enforced in all Nazi-occupied countries, and disobedience resulted in imprisonment. In the name of ethnic cleansing, these camps were set up for the country's Sinti, Roma, Jews, the disabled, believers of other religions, homosexuals, and people who openly criticized Nazi Germany's policies (communists and socialists). Furthermore, German avant-garde writers, artists, designers, and teachers whose works were considered "degenerate art" that disturbed the social order were also suppressed. Between 1933 and 1945, approximately 180,000–220,000 European refugees are said to have fled and emigrated to the United States to escape Nazi rule, although figures vary depending on the data.[13]

The camp uniforms included color-coded badges to distinguish between the various people in the camps. Figue 8.5 is a color chart of the camp insignia created by the Nazi SS in 1938. A facsimile of it is currently on display in the Topography of Terror Museum in Berlin, built on the site of the former headquarters of the Secret State Police (Gestapo). The colors were assigned according to the reason for their detention and further classified into several subcategories. Inmates were wearing color badges indicating their categories in two spots—on the left chest and on the right leg area of the camp uniform, which resembled the striped pajamas depicted in the lower right corner of Figure 8.5. The

Fig. 8.4 A yellow patch to distinguish Jews (*Source* Auschwitz Peace Museum, Fukushima, Japan)

---

[13] https://exhibitions.ushmm.org/americans-and-the-holocaust/how-many-refugees-came-to-the-united-states-from-1933-1945.

yellow Jewish six-pointed Star of David was particularly conspicuous (Fig. 8.5). The use of this hexagram made up of yellow triangles, a well-known Jewish identification symbol, has a long history in the Middle East and Europe. The yellow badge is believed to have been introduced into the Muslim empire by the Umayyad caliph Umar II in the early eighth century as a color for Jewish identification. It has been used in the Muslim and Christian worlds since the Middle Ages. In 1121, the following decree was recorded in a synagogue document:

Two yellow badges must be displayed, one on the hat and one on the neck.[14]

Yellow is the color of the Chinese emperors and the symbol of gold in European heraldry. However, for Nazi Germany, yellow and the six-pointed star were symbols of Jewish persecution. In some German states, Jews were forced to always wear a yellow six-pointed star on their clothing even before they were sent to camps. The Nazi Party public relations newspaper *Parole der Woche* (*Slogan of the Week*) used the color badge to incite racial hatred ("Whoever wears this yellow six-pointed star is our enemy").[15]

In the 2000 American-Canadian TV mini-series *Nuremberg*, based on the book *Nuremberg: Infamy on Trial*, which depicts the trials of war criminals in Nazi Germany, a Jewish officer of the American army asks the most important defendant, Hermann Wilhelm Göring (1893–1946), "Did you have no scruples in slaughtering people of Jewish descent?" He responded that it was no different from the situation in the United States, where Japanese had been interned and blacks were discriminated against. James Whitman, a comparative and criminal law professor at Yale Law School, explained how the Nazis created a framework for racial discrimination modeled on American racial discrimination laws.[16] He justified the discriminatory policies of the Nuremberg Laws using the precedent of discrimination against people of color in immigration law in the United States, especially the cases of deprivation of voting rights and interracial marriages. In other words, the Nazis conducted the Holocaust guided by already existing race-based American laws.

[14] Johnson, P. (1988). *A History of the Jews*, pp. 204–205.

[15] *Parole der Woche* (1942, July 1).

[16] Whitman, J. Q. (2017). Hitler's American Model: The United States and the Making of Nazi Race Law. (No. 1165/4267) [Kindle].

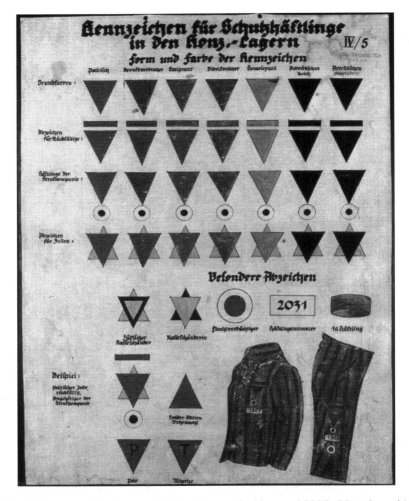

Fig. 8.5 Instructional material for SS guards (*Source* 25305 ©Bundesarchiv, Koblenz, 146-1993-051-07. *Note* Concentration camp insignia for protective custody prisoners: from 1938, prisoners were categorized by reason for detention and race, with further individual subcategories. Header, from left: Political: Professional Criminal: Emigrant: Jehovah's Witnesses: Homosexual: Work-shy Reich: Work-shy Municipalities. Left column from above: Basic Colors, Insignia for Recidivists: Prisoners of the Punishment Battalion, Insignia for Jews: There follow Special Insignia. From left: Jewish Race Defiler: Female Race Defiler: Suspected Fugitive: Prisoner Number: 1A Prisoner. Example: Political Jew, Recidivist, Member of the Punishment Battalion: Wehrmacht Special Operation: P is Polish: T is Czech)

8.3 WHITE, BLACK, AND RED

Jew me, sue me
Everybody, do me
Kick me, kike me
Don't you black or white me
Michael Jackson, *They Don't Care About US* (1995).[17]

The promotional video for the prison version of Michael Jackson's (1958–2009) song "*They Don't Care About US*" features scenes of prison and police violence in the United States. Michael Jackson, the top African-American singer and King of Pop, underwent repeated plastic surgery, bleached his skin, and became biracial in appearance from the 1990s onward. He lived in a world where people were judged, categorized, and oppressed based on their skin color. In the conclusion of the previous chapter, I discussed that Nazi Germany based its race-based laws, which culminated in genocide, on America's racist Jim Crow laws. In this chapter, I would like to consider how the basic color terms that appear earliest—black, white, and red—have divided human beings; it might have been an inevitability and not an accident that the infamous Nazi swastika flag was black, white, and red. In this section, I will explain how laws dividing human beings by skin color came about.

8.3.1 Black and White

First, let me introduce the associations with the color black, which are widespread in English-speaking cultures. In a book of essays on color terms, the linguist and literary scholar Sandford conducted a study using the Implicit Association Test (IAT), a psychology test. The IAT revealed that the concepts associated with the English words black and white are not pleasant and white, respectively.[18] Since ancient times, the English language has used white to mean good and black to mean evil. For

---

[17] http://www.nextenglish.net/they-dont-care-about-us-michael-jackson.

[18] Sandford, J. L. (2018). "Black and White Linguistic Category Entrenchment in English." In L. W. MacDonald, C. P. Biggam, & G. V. Paramei (Eds.), *Progress in Colour Studies: Cognition, Language and Beyond*, pp. 269–283.

160   K. HIDAKA

example, there are words such as blacklist[19] and blackmail, and Sandford's results showed that this tradition has continued into modern times.

For further information on the meaning and symbolism of the color black, see the research by Van Norden[20] and Pastoureau.[21] The meanings of black in Europe have been classified by Pastoureau as follows.

1. Color of death.
   Hell, devil, darkness, mourning, funeral or mourning clothes, black cloth. Color of misfortune.
2. Color of error, sin, and dishonesty.
   The opposite of white, the symbol of purity and virginity. The color of the dirty and defiled (grime, dust). The color of hatred. Black flag. Anarchy. Nihilism. The "black shirt" (the Italian fascist uniform). Violence, fascism, totalitarianism.
   Punishment, prison, solitary confinement, Post Office Cryptography Room (*Cabinet noir* in French).
3. Color of sadness, loneliness, and melancholy.
   Gloomy thoughts, brooding thoughts, pessimism.
   Young people who like black. The color of old age, senility, and endings (in contrast, white is the color of beginnings). The color of fear, dark movies. Dark novels. Dark atmosphere.
4. Color of religion, piety, rigor, renunciation of worldly pleasures.
   Clothing of monastic and parochial clergy. The "crow" (priest in black).
   The color of modesty, reserve, and moderation. Protestant. Puritan strictness.
5. Color of fashion.
   Black clothes, black ties, and black dresses, a color of elegance and modernity.
   Ceremonial pomp. Luxury goods. Depth and wealth. Artists who prefer black. Design, avant-garde. Sophisticated gift packaging and wrapping.

[19] Charles II called the list of 58 judges who sentenced his father, King Charles I, to death in the Puritan Revolution a blacklist.

[20] Van Norden, L. (1985). *The Black Feet of the Peacock: The Color-Concept 'Black' from the Greeks Through the Renaissance.*

[21] Pastoureau, M. (2008). *Black: The History of a Color.*

8 CATEGORIZING PEOPLE BY COLOR 161

6. Color of authority.

Sports referee, judge, and jailer. In the past, soldiers, firefighters, and police officers.[22]

Black derives from the word *bhleg*, which comes from Indo-European sources, meaning "to burn with black smoke" or "to burn black with smoke."[23] The *Oxford English Dictionary* states that black began to indicate "foul, wicked iniquitous, diabolical atrocious, terribly malicious wicked" in the late sixteenth century (c. 1581).[24] Thus, the history of the English language shows that the tendency to bring to the fore negative feelings, which could be called discrimination, toward black became more pronounced from around the sixteenth century.

These feelings toward black did not develop overnight. How exactly do negative feelings toward the color black appear in ancient literature? In Western European culture, white and black have traditionally symbolized good and evil (figuratively associated with light and darkness, day and night), and the dichotomy between light and darkness is already expressed in the table of opposites created by the ancient Greek Pythagorean school.[25] In the sixteenth and seventeenth centuries, witch hunts were commonplace, and black was also associated with witchcraft based on evil intentions, as in black magic or evil spells.

In the strange novel *Pantagruel, The Very Horrific Life of Great Gargantua, Father of Pantagruel* by the French Renaissance humanist François Rabelais, the giant Gargantua begins to explain that the colors that represent his status are white and blue. White is the color of joy, and its opposite, black, is the color of sorrow. Then, he notes that the concepts come from Aristotle's teachings and that those who wish to express sorrow wear black garments.[26]

---

[22] Pastoureau, M. (1995). *Colors of Europe*, pp. 72–74.

[23] *Bhleg* was incorporated into Old High German as *blah* (black), Low Franconian as 'black' (ink) and Old Norse as *blakkr* (dark, dusky). 'black' (ink) and Old Norse as *blakkr* (dark, dusky). Is this a citation of the original work? Why not show only the source?

[24] *The Oxford English Dictionary, Second Edition* (1989). Clarendon Press. Definition 9, p. 239.

[25] The Pythagorean school of philosophy expresses the properties of ten pairs of opposites. The earliest reference is found in Aristotle's *Metaphysics*.

[26] Rabelais. (1991). *Rabelais's First Book: Pantagruel, The Very Horrific Life of Great Gargantua, Father of Pantagruel*, Japanese translation, pp. 70–77.

162   K. HIDAKA

I would like to look at the meaning of the color black in England as expressed in several plays by William Shakespeare (1564–1616):

1. *Titus Andronicus*   Act I. Then two men bearing a coffin covered with *black*[27]

2. *Timon of Athens*   Act IV, Scene 3
Timon: *Black* white, foul fair, wrong right[28]

3. *Henry VIII*   Act I. The King, Hath into monstrous habits put the graces, that once were his, and is become as *black*, as if besmeared in hell[29]

4. *Macbeth*   Act I. My *black* and deep desires[30]

5. *Hamlet*   Act 3, Scene 2.
Hamlet: So long? Nay, then, let the devil wear *black*.[31]

In these examples from Shakespeare's plays, black is depicted as the color of death, ugliness, evil, lowliness, old age, and cowardice, a color that evokes all negative words. The spread of English from one regional language in northern Europe, particularly England, to the rest of the world also spread the worldview of the language. In the history of England, there is a man called the Black Prince, Edward of Woodstock (1330–1376), who was said to be so-called because he always wore black armor, although there is also a theory that the French called him *L'Homme Noir* in response to his atrocities.

After Shakespeare's time, playwright Thomas Middleton (1580–1627) allegedly coined the notion of "whites" in his 1613 play *The Triumphs of Truth*.[32] Prior to that, a play called *Masque of Blackness* (1600), performed at the Jacobean court in England, told the story of women who arrived at the royal court for King James to "purify" them of their blackness. The darker-skinned race was considered corrupt, and the white

---

[27] Shakespeare, *Titus Andronicus* (1593–1594).

[28] Shakespeare, *Timon of Athens* (1607–1608).

[29] Shakespeare, *Henry VIII* (1612–1613).

[30] Shakespeare, *Macbeth* (1606).

[31] Shakespeare, *Hamlet* (c. 1599–1601).

[32] https://aeon.co/ideas/how-white-people-were-invented-by-a-playwright-in-1613.

race was pure.[33] Even as late as the twentieth century, some British politicians believed that the African race of "Black Africa" could not rule rationally and justly.[34] The judgment that white = good and black = evil exists in many cultures, but the hierarchy of white on top and black at the bottom, the propagation of the notion that "mixing colors" is evil, dividing people by skin color, and assigning superiority or inferiority are prominent in European language cultures. These ideals are also projected onto the color system.

8.3.2 Redlining

Since the abolition of slavery in Portugal in the eighteenth century, slavery has been gradually abolished around the world, bringing to light the racism that disadvantages people because of the color of their skin. In this context, the racism embedded in the English language itself was discussed and gradually changed through protests and social conditions. For example, when the *Dictionary of Color Standards* was published in by the BCC in 1934, "Nigger Brown" was originally listed as a color. However, with the growing influence of the American civil rights and anti-racism movements of the 1950s and 1960s, the 1961 edition changed the term for this color to "African Brown" (Fig. 8.6).[35]

The Jim Crow laws of the United States to which the Nazis referred were a series of harsh racial discrimination laws in the southern states of the United States that existed from 1876 to 1964 and collectively concerned the segregation and disenfranchisement of people of color. Whites living in the South legislated the persecution of people of color after slavery was banned after the Civil War. White supremacy was threatened by their defeat, and whites tried to protect their former "master" status by threatening African Americans who tried to exercise their rights with laws and police powers.[36] The persecution of the Jim Crow laws was

---

[33] McDermott, K. (2002). *"To Blanch an Ethiop": Jonson's Masque of Blackness and Multicultural English Literature*, p. 20.

[34] Robbins, K. (Ed.). (2013). *Oxford History of the British Isles 10–20th Century 1901–1951*, p. 64.

[35] Hidaka, K. (2018). *Official British Traditional Colours Listed by the British Colour Council*, p. 108.

[36] Appiah, A., & Gates, H. L., Jr. (1999). *Africana: The Encyclopedia of the African and African American Experience*, p. 1211.

Fig. 8.6 British Colour Council, notes on corrections in the 1961 reprint of the Dictionary of Colour Standards (*Source* University Library for Agricultural and Life Sciences, the University of Tokyo. *Note* In its original publication in 1934, BCC20 African Brown was originally spelled using a term considered racist towards Africans. As a response to the growing global protests against racial discrimination and the American Civil Rights Movement of the 1950s and 1960s, the offensive term was removed from the name in 1961)

not only against "African Negroes" but against all non-whites (known as coloreds, e.g., Natives, Mexicans, and persons of mixed race) based on the one-drop rule that all persons with any mixed blood shall be considered Negroes. In schools, buses, trains, restaurants, movie theaters, etc., white people and people of color were separated by skin color and could not be seated together. Mixed-race marriages between white and colored were also not allowed. Even if they wanted to oppose this, people of color were disenfranchised and deprived of the right to vote. Violence against people of color by police officers was also permitted.

A vestige of the Jim Crow laws and structural racism against people of color is redlining, a form of economic oppression unique to the United States; it is the practice of making it harder for residents of certain neighborhoods to obtain mortgages, insurance, credit cards, and other financial services based on race or ethnicity. The name "redlining" comes from the fact that financial institutions would outline black neighborhoods in red on their lending maps. In other words, redlining is a form of discrimination that divides housing environments by race. The value of homes in redlined neighborhoods is less than half that of homes in areas that the government considered "optimal" for mortgage financing, and this oppression predates the specific enforcement that began with the National Housing Act of 1934 and the establishment of the Federal Housing Administration.

Redlining of areas based on race is now officially illegal (redlining for areas with ostensibly geologically unstable ground, volcanoes, flooding, and other problems is, of course, still legal). However, many residential neighborhoods that are still predominantly populated by people of color have been redlined areas for over 100 years; real estate prices are lower in these areas, making houses harder to sell; loan interest and homeowners' insurance rates are higher than those for whites, which also makes houses harder to buy. Schools in districts in redlined areas are usually poorer and face multiple disadvantages compared with better-funded schools in markers such as college entrance exam scores.[37] In addition, neighborhood redlining can affect public health; parks and welfare facilities in urban areas, predominantly communities of color, are likely to be smaller and of lower quality than those in wealthier, predominantly white neighborhoods. The overall result of all these factors is that residents of redlined neighborhoods face considerably greater barriers to success than do residents of middle-class or upscale areas, such as lower property values and higher interest rates, poor credit, poor health and safety and fewer overall opportunities for success in life.[38] In the twenty-first century the scars of the color-based racism that began with 16th-century oppression and persecution based on skin color still remain.[39]

---

[37] In the US, college admissions are often determined by SAT or ACT scores, high school transcripts, and interviews, with transcripts given weight according to high school rankings.

[38] https://www.cbsnews.com/news/redlining-what-is-history-mike-bloomberg-comments/ (Accessed: April 24, 2021).

[39] Rothstein, R. (2017). *The Color of Law: A Forgotten History of How Our Government Segregated America* (1st ed.), Preface.

8.3.3 #BlackLivesMatter

The BLM protest movement began with the hashtag #Black Lives Matter or #BLM on various social networking sites in 2013. The movement grew worldwide following the incident in which an African-American man, George Floyd, was choked to death by a white police officer in Minneapolis, Minnesota, at the end of May 2020, and the video of the incident was broadcast on the internet. The incident triggered a massive global protest against violent acts and structural racism by white police officers that persists throughout the United States.

Two of the most famous slogans of the BLM movement are "I can't breathe" and "Silence is violence." The former was the final appeal of two victims of police violence, Eric Garner in New York in 2014 and George Floyd in 2020, who were both choked to death; at both sites, there were people taking videos, but no one stopped the violence of the police officers. The latter phrase symbolizes that silence in the face of unreasonable violence by police officers leads to new victims.

The video evidence of police brutality has taken over the world and even changed daily language. For instance, in programming terminology, one outcome of the BLM movement was that GitHub revisited the terms "master/slave" and "blacklist/whitelist." Just as we are correcting what has traditionally reflected racism at the level of the color words we unconsciously use, so should the discriminatory expressions used in our daily lives be changed in the future. For instance, loan color names used in Japanese, such as "black company," and "black school rules," which have become Japanese-English words, have become commonly used without due consideration. We all need to be aware of the latent discrimination in the color terms we utter, the logic of the color system, and other ideas about why we sort colors in this way, and to continue to speak out and make changes.

8.3.4 Silence Is Violence

As my hope for the world, I would like to conclude this chapter with a high-profile victory in protesting violence against skin color. Naomi Osaka (1997–), a Japanese national whose father was born in Haiti and whose mother is Japanese, is a professional tennis player with an illustrious history of winning the US and Australian Opens. In tennis, a sport of white upper-class society, she has been one of the best in the world.

At the end of August 2020, a black man, Jacob Blake, was shot seven times from behind by a white police officer in Wisconsin in the United States. In protest against the repeated assaults and murders of blacks by police officers, a boycott of basketball games was first called by the National Basketball Association (NBA), which has a high percentage of black players. In response to the NBA's action, Osaka announced that she would withdraw from the Western and Southern Open tournament, in which she had advanced to the semifinals. The US Tennis Association respected Osaka's wishes and postponed the semifinals. Some people criticized her decision to withdraw, saying, "Don't mix politics and sport," meaning "Blacks should shut up and play sports instead of complaining about being slaughtered by white police officers." These people are not only unaware of the daily oppression and violence against nonwhite Americans but also do not realize that most *Nikkei* and Asians have a hard time taking their place at the political and academic center of society.

Rather than succumbing to these criticisms, Osaka embodied the value of calling out the victims of oppression and violence worldwide. In 2020, she competed in the US Open, making statements with black masks required by COVID-19 (the disease caused by the novel coronavirus that required people to wear infection-prevention masks in public), each of which bore in white letters the name of a different black victim of racist US police violence in white letters, in every round of the tournament. She vowed to win the US Open to show the world the names of the following victims:

Breonna Taylor
Elijah McCain
Ahmaud Arbery
Trayvon Martin
George Floyd (final round).[40]

---

[40] BBC September 9, 2020, News. https://www.bbc.com/news/world-us-canada-540 88453.

8.4 Stereotypes in Film: White Saviors and Magical Negroes

As the saying goes, a picture is worth a thousand words. The videos of emaciated corpses in concentration camps, which the Nazi government had taken as records, were shown as definitive evidence at the long-running Nuremberg military trials from November 20, 1945, to October 1, 1946. The videos presented evidence of the crimes committed under the Nazi regime, and the major defendants were convicted.

Movies started to spread when the American inventor Edison devised the first idea for a movie-viewing device called a kinetoscope in 1888. Until the end of the nineteenth century, the kinetoscope displayed dozens of still images or photographs per second that differed slightly from one another like a flipbook, tricking the eye into thinking the images were moving and projecting them onto a screen as an application of optical illusion. Later, movies (motion pictures, film, and video) spread as a medium that presented storylines with solid emotional appeal through the synergy of music and actors' performances. Around World War I, the movies rapidly assumed an important position as a form of entertainment and documentation.

Stereotypes existed and continue to exist in the Hollywood film industry, in which roles are cast according to skin color. These stereotypes include the "white savior" and the "magical negro." In a white savior movie, a white person plays the good guy, and the "magical negro" plays the role of a wizard who helps the white protagonist in a crisis, often with impossible physical abilities or wisdom. Critics argue that because these stereotypes have been widely released as cinematic works, viewers have been instilled with a sense of hierarchy as in a master–servant relationship.

Nigerian American novelist Teju Cole (1975–) coined the term "White Savior Industrial Complex."[41] The term criticizes white celebrity singers and film actors for their philanthropic and human rights appeals, such as adopting African children. These activities, Cole explains, are promoted with an emphasis on helping the disadvantaged but ignore the systems and policies of oppression of people of color that whites have maintained

---

[41] Aronson, A. (2017). "The White Savior Industrial Complex: A Cultural Studies Analysis of a Teacher Educator, Savior Film, and Future Teachers." *Journal of Critical Thought and Praxis*, 6(3), pp. 36–54.

as if they did not exist. Here I present a list of 35 films or television shows—among many, many possibilities—that I think most vividly depict the color categorization and the struggle against discrimination on film:

1. *Roots* (1977)
2. *Gandhi* (1982)
3. *The Color Purple* (1985)
4. *Cry Freedom* (1987)
5. *Mississippi Burning* (1988)
6. *Do the Right Thing* (1989)
7. *Paris Is Burning* (1990)
8. *Malcolm X* (1992)
9. *A Time to Kill* (1996)
10. *Amistad* (1997)
11. *Hairspray* (2007)
12. *Goodbye Bafana* (2007)
13. *The Secret Life of Bees* (2008)
14. *Invictus* (2009)
15. *The Help* (2011)
16. *The Butler* (2013)
17. *Fruitvale Station* (2013)
18. *Orange Is the New Black* (2013–2019)
19. *12 Years a Slave* (2013)
20. *Belle* (2013)
21. *Selma* (2015)
22. *13th* (2016)
23. *Hidden Figures* (2016)
24. *Fences* (2016)
25. *Detroit* (2017)
26. *I Am Not Your Negro* (2017)
27. Kings (2017)
28. *Victoria & Abdul* (2017)
29. *Where Hands Touch* (2018)
30. *BlackKklansman* (2018)
31. *The Hate U Give* (2018)
32. *Green Book* (2018)
33. *Watchmen* (2019)
34. *When They See Us* (2019)
35. *If Beale Street Could Talk* (2019)

PART III

Epilogue

CHAPTER 9

Conclusion—A Past That Ranks Colors and Refuses to Mix, and a Colorful Future

October 8, 1786. It is evident that the eye forms itself by the objects, which, from youth up, it is accustomed to look upon.
    Goethe, *Goethe's Travels in Italy*.[1]

I believe that people gradually learn color categorization from childhood and that living environments, education, and laws shape the framework of human categorization. The standards of color categorization we learn while growing up weave the "color culture." The academic trend in color culture is illustrated by *A Cultural History of Color*, published in six volumes at the end of 2020 by Bloomsbury Publishing.[2] The series, compiled by linguists Carole P. Biggam and Kirsten Wolf, is notable for pieces that trace the phenomenon of color from Western history, science and technology, politics, art, and linguistic expression.

The perspective of diversity is essential to the study of colorful cultures. Differences in lighting preferred by different regions, vegetation, history, and languages are the sources of the earth's colorful cultures. Due to the difficulty of studying all these under the same uniform standards

---

[1] von Goethe, J. W. (1885). Goethe's Travels in Italy: Together with His Second Residence in Rome and Fragments on Italy (Alexander James William Morrison, A.J.W. et al. Trans.). G. Bell and sons.

[2] Biggam, C. P., & Wolf, K. (2020). *A Cultural History of Color*.

© The Author(s), under exclusive license to Springer Nature Switzerland AG 2024
K. Hidaka, *The Art of Color Categorization*,
https://doi.org/10.1007/978-3-031-47690-7_9

173

174   K. HIDAKA

and conditions, some people ask me, "Isn't this standardized?" However, there will always be human universals. Based on these criteria, I believe the ideal approach to color culture research is to examine universal commonalities versus differences.

At this point, I am taking the view of modest cultural universals. I believe most humans have a universal trichromatic (red, blue, yellow) vision, a biological mechanism common to all human beings, along with life, death, gender, eating, sleeping, reproduction, and excretion. In contrast, culture, customs, and language create variations depending on the environment in which human beings grow up.

When I visited my grandmother, then in her nineties and intermittently in a critical condition, in hospital, my uncle told me: Humans have a death rate of 100%. Irrespective of medical care, hygiene, stress, or diet, most humans have a life span of 70–90 years, and everyone will die. In his book *Where did Humanity Come From: An Approach from Primate Studies*, primatologist Nishida argued that the view that education and culture can change humans is "pouring out harmful poison."[3] Nishida's view that human and primate behavior is based on innate biological traits is reasonable, but education and culture can also influence behavior, and behavior changes when the environment changes.

As for myself, I think that the traditional colors and color schemes that are typical of my culture, including the criteria for color categorization, have been nurtured mainly through food culture—daily food, festivals, food preparation—and seasonal events. In my daily life, familiar landscapes, food, people's skin and hair, and memories of accumulated colors and shapes create colors that are unique to my environment.

While living in different environments on the earth, each person learns what is important to them. My path started with my eating habits and the bright colors of Jewish and Italian cakes in New York, from which I became curious about how other people see and feel what I felt daily, which led me to this book. As the basic hardware of a human being installs over time the software of color categorization standards and language depending on their living environment, unique color cultures are fostered, and individual differences in hardware in environments give rise to diversity. However, as long as the hardware is human, diversity is not a clash

---

[3] Nishida, T. (2007). *Where Did Humanity Come From: An Approach from Primate Studies*. Kyoto University Press, p. 302.

9 CONCLUSION—A PAST THAT RANKS COLORS AND REFUSES … 175

of dissimilarities. Rather, we should always deepen our understanding of and respect for each other.

Humans have the concept of color and generally to some extent classify red, blue, etc. in a similar way. Otherwise, how could we translate and understand them? This hypothesis was the starting point for the theory of cultural universals, which begins with Berlin and Kay's *Basic Color Terms*. In this book, I have reviewed color naming, color vision, the translation of color names, bilingualism, and color charts for research, focusing on what I could not write in the translator's postscript of *Basic Color Terms*.

Color categorization and Darwinism are closely connected. The discussion of Basic Color Terms, the development of color charts, and scientific support for the view of race are evolutionary theories. The sorting of plants and animals based on Darwinian evolutionary theory was further developed in humans, leading to eugenics in the early twentieth century and the use of color charts to discriminate based on race. In the upper elementary school grades, I read *The Diary of Anne Frank* and wondered why a girl in her teens had to run away, hide with her family, live in attics, etc., and then be killed in a camp because she was Jewish. Similarly, listening to the news when the apartheid policy was in effect in South Africa, I wondered why people had to live in separate places because of their skin color. I spent most of my teens in the United States. Although I did not experience tragic persecution like Anne Frank or a policy like apartheid, I was forced to learn the reality of racism based on skin color. I became aware of conflicts about color (race) all over the world through the friction caused when people rank others according to the color of their skin or eyes, or when mixed marriage is prohibited.

Identifying the fat content of milk using red, green, or blue color markings on the packaging is convenient. However, color-coding people based on skin color or other attributes leads to hatred, violence, and murder. At an academic meeting on classification, historian Masayuki Yamauchi questioned whether dividing residential areas is the notion of sedentary peoples, especially European and Chinese agricultural peoples.[4] Humans might have come to divide things to show their ownership and confirm their status in the land, including their superiority with their ethnicity. It is because we live in an environment where colors are scarce,

---

[4] Yamauchi, M. (2001). Separating Nation from Nation? Lessons for the 20th Century, p. 6. Collection of essays based on public lectures. University of Tokyo Sogo Kenkyukai (Ed.). (2001). *Dividing (Wakeru, University of Tokyo Open Lecture 73)*.

rather than abundant, that we are so particular about colors. Categorizing colors results from people living in an environment that requires detailed categorization and who use such categorization to communicate with others.

Communication is the sharing of information, ideas, and thoughts with others. Since 2019, I have had the opportunity to co-sponsor a joint workshop with Assumption University in Thailand to create digital art. Seeing students from more than ten different countries enjoying the interaction of machines with vivid, colorful lights and sounds, I observed that everyone reacts in the same way and finds more or less the same things interesting, and just as what we find interesting is similar, what we find painful should be as well. I want to remind my readers that it is also painful for all human beings to be judged, discriminated against, and disadvantaged based on the color of their skin. Hopefully, this book will contribute to a future with a more sensitive worldview and mutual understanding in the face of all kinds of unreasonable discrimination.

REFERENCES

Andrews, D. R. (1994). The Russian Color Categories Sinij and Goluboj: An Experimental Analysis of Their Interpretation in the Standard and Émigré Languages. *Journal of Slavic linguistics, 2*(1), (pp. 9–28).

Appiah, A., & Gates, H. L., Jr. (1999). *Africana: the encyclopedia of the African and African American experience.* Basic Civitas Books.

Arihara, K. (2014). 'White Food' and 'Red Food' in Mongolia. *Bulletin of the Tohoku Animal Science and Technology Society, 64*(1), (pp. 1–6).

Aronson, B. (2017). The White Savior Industrial Complex: A Cultural Studies Analysis of a Teacher Educator Savior Film and Future Teachers. *Journal of Critical Thought and Praxis 6(3),* https://doi.org/10.31274/jctp-180 810-83

Baines, J. (1985). Color Terminology and Color Classification: Ancient Egyptian Color Terminology and Polychromy. *American Anthropologist, 87*(2), (pp. 282–297).

Baker, G. (2019). *Rainbow Warrior: My Life in Color.* Chicago Review Press.

Benczes, R., & Tóth-Czifra, E. (2014). The Hungarian Colour Terms piros and vörös. *Acta Linguistica Hungarica, 61*, (pp. 123–152).

Berlin, B., & Kay, P. (1969). *Basic Color Terms: Their Universality and Evolution.* University of California Press.

Berlin, B., & Kay, P. (1999). *Basic Color Terms: Their Universality and Evolution* (The David Hume series, philosophy and cognitive science reissues). Center for the Study of Language and Information.

Biggam, C. P. (1997). *Blue in Old English: An Interdisciplinary Semantic Study* (Vol. 110). Rodopi.

© The Editor(s) (if applicable) and The Author(s), under exclusive license to Springer Nature Switzerland AG 2024
K. Hidaka, *The Art of Color Categorization,*
https://doi.org/10.1007/978-3-031-47690-7

178 REFERENCES

Biggam, C. P. (2012). *The Semantics of Colour: A Historical Approach.* Cambridge: Cambridge University Press.

Biggam, C. P., &. Paramei G. V. (Eds.). (2006). *Progress in Colour Studies: Volume I. Language and Culture.* John Benjamins Publishing Company.

Biggam, C. P., et al. (2020). *A Cultural History of Color.* Bloomsbury Academic.

Blaszczyk, R. L. (2012). *The Color Revolution.* The MIT Press.

Blumenbach, J. F. (1795). *De generis humani varietate native* (Natural Variation of Human). Göttingen: Vandenhoek & Ruprecht.

Boyatzis, C. J., & Varghese, R. (1994). Children's Emotional Associations with Colors. *The Journal of Genetic Psychology: Research and Theory on Human Development, 155*(1), (pp. 77–85).

Boyne, J. (2008). *The Boy in the Striped Pajamas* (Shigeki Chiba, Trans.). Iwanami Shoten.

Brown, D. E. (2002). *Human Universals: From Cultural Relativism to the Recognition of Universality* (Kotaro Suzuki & Kiyoshi Nakamura, Trans.). Shinyosha.

Brown, P. (2014). *Red Rising.* Del Rey Books.

Burleigh, M., & Wippermann, W. (1991). *The Racial State: Germany 1933–1945.* Cambridge University Press.

Caivano, J. L., & Nemcsics, A. (2022). Color Order Systems. In R. Shamey (Ed.), *Encyclopedia of Color Science and Technology.* Berlin, Heidelberg: Springer.

Central Weather Bureau and Marine Observatory (Eds.). (1976). *Weather History of Japan 2, Vol. 11: "Rainbows and Halo",* (pp. 655–665). Hara Shobō.

The Color Science Society of Japan. (2006). *Color in Life,* edited by *Color Science Course 2.* Asakura Shoten.

Conklin, H. C. (1955). Hanunóo Color Categories. *Southwestern Journal of Anthropology, 11*(4), (pp. 339–344).

Conklin, H. C. (1999). Hanunóo Color Categories—Rethinking Classification. *Journal of Ethno-natural History, Ecosophia, (3),* (pp. 89–93).

Cytowic, R. E. (2003). *The Man Who Tasted Shapes* (Yamashita, A. Trans.). Soshisha.

Da Vinci, L., Rigaud, J. F., & Brown, W. B. A. (1892). *Treatise on Painting.* General Remarks on Colours. George Bell & Sons.

Deflem, M. (1991). Ritual, Anti-structure, and Religion: A Discussion of Victor Turner's Processual Symbolic Analysis. *Journal for the Scientific Study of Religion, 30*(1), (pp. 1–25).

Deutscher, G. (2011). *Through the Language Glass: Why The World Looks Different In Other Languages.* Arrow (2012, Naoko Mukuta, Trans.). Intershift.

Everett, D. L. (2009). *Don't Sleep, There Are Snakes: Life and Language in the Amazonian Jungle.* Knopf Doubleday Publishing Group.

REFERENCES 179

Friedman, B. (1931). The Blue Arcs of the Retina. *Archives of Ophthalmology*, *6*(5), (pp. 663–674).

Fujiwara No Michitoshi Compiled. (1086). *Goshūi Wakashū*.

Fukuda, K. (1999). *Where Did the Names of Colors Come from—Their Meanings and Culture*. Seiga Shobō.

Fukuda, K. (2012). *New Edition: Dictionary of Color Names 507--From History to Miscellaneous Information and Color Data, Japanese and World Colors Can Be Seen, Read, and Understood*. Shufunotomo.

Fukui, K. (1977). 'Color' and 'Pattern' of the Bodi People: The World of Pastoralists, Southwestern Ethiopia. *Ethnology Quarterly, 2*, (pp. 36–49).

Fukui, K. (1978). The Symbolic World of Color and Pattern in Pastoral Society: The Bodi People of Ethiopia. *The World of Creation, 25*, (pp. 48–79).

Fukui, K. (1991). *Recognition and Culture: An Ethnography of Color and Pattern*. University of Tokyo Press.

Fukuzawa, Y. (1869). *Shochu bankoku ichiran (Pocket Almanac of the World)*, Fukuzawa Zohan. Keio University Library. https://dcollections.lib.keio.ac.jp/ja/fukuzawa/a10/29

Gage, J. (1999). *Color and Culture*. University of California Press.

Gleason, H. A. (Originally 1961). Introduction to Descriptive Linguistics. (1970, co-trans. by Takebayashi and Yokoyama). Daishukan Shoten.

Goethe, J. (1885). *Goethe's Travels in Italy: Together with His Second Residence in Rome and Fragments on Italy* (Alexander James William Morrison, A.J.W. et al. Trans.). G. Bell and sons. Classical Culture Library (Koten Kyoyo Bunko).

Goethe, J. W. V. (1840). *Theory of Colours* (C. Lock Eastlake, Trans.; 1st ed.). Routledge. (1999, Takahashi et al. Trans. Kōsakusha)

Hachijo, T. (2020). *Illustrated Guide to the Colors of Yushoku: Japanese Traditional Colors*. Tankōsha.

Hankins, T. L. (1994). The Ocular Harpsichord of Louis-Bertrand Castel; or, the Instrument That Wasn't. *Osiris, 9*, (pp. 141–156).

Hardin, C. L., & Maffi, L. (1997). *Color Categories in Thought and Language*. Cambridge University Press.

Hariman, R. (1992). Decorum, Power, and the Courtly Style. *Quarterly Journal of Speech, 78*(2), (pp. 149–172).

Hayakawa, M. (2000). Color Image of Milk Packages of Various Companies–Symbolism of Color. *Sanno University Bulletin*, (pp. 333–338).

Henrich, J. (2016). *The Secret of Our Success: How Culture Is Driving Human Evolution, Domesticating Our Species, and Making Us Smarter*. Princeton University Press. (Y. Imanishi, Trans.). Hakuyosha.

Hidaka, K. (2001). *A Cultural Historical Study of Gold and Black Colour in the Embroidery of Late Sixteenth to Early Seventeenth Century England*. Doctoral Thesis, Tokyo University of the Arts.

180 REFERENCES

Hidaka, K. (2015). A Comparative Cultural Study of Colors and Designs of Milk Packages in Japan and the United States. *Bulletin of Tama Art University, 30*, (pp. 155–163).

Hidaka, K. (2016). A Comparison of Color Schemes and Images in the Package Design of Sweets in the US and Japan. *Cultura E Scienza Del Colore—Color Culture and Science, 5*, (pp. 7–14).

Hidaka, K. (2017). Categorization of Japanese Traditional Color Scheme into 'Hare-Ke': An Attempt from View of Food Culture. *Journal of the Color Science Association of Japan, 41(3+)*, (pp. 34–35).

Hidaka, K. (2020). Re-examining "Basic Color Terms": Color Charts and Lighting. *Journal of the Color Science Association of Japan, 44*(4), (pp. 176–179).

Hidaka, K. (2021). What Is Color Order System? *Information Science and Technology, 71*(3), (pp. 101–106).

Hidaka, T. (1984). *Inu no Kotoba (The Language of Dogs)*. Seidosha.

Hirasawa, Y. (1997). The Problem of Cultural Development Degree from the Viewpoint of Color. *Journal of the Society for Information and Culture, 4*(1), (pp. 17–26).

Hirayama, S. (2018). *The Pictorial Book of Japanese Military Uniforms: Meiji Period*. Kokushokan.

Shimada, H. (2016). *History of Religious Events as a Culture*. Kawade Shobo Shinsha.

Hidaka, K. (2018). Official British Traditional Colours Listed by the British Colour Council. *Journal of the Color Science Association of Japan, 42*(3+), p. 108.

Hisano, A. (2019). *Visualizing Taste: How Business Changed the Look of What You Eat*. Harvard University Press.

Hitler, A. ([1925–26].1973, Hirano & Shozumi, Trans.). *Mein Kampf* (Vol. 1). Kadokawa.

Ibuki, T. (2005). *Package Strategy 110 Articles: A Book Connecting Managers, Marketing Men, and Designers, Part 1*. Nippo Shuppan.

Iehara, M. (1876). *Irozu Mondou*. Shiga Shinbun.

Itagaki, A., & Okuda, S. (2011). Research on color of wrapping paper in Japanese-style confection shop in Kyoto. *Doshisha Women's University Life Science, 45*, (pp. 60–63).

Itakura, K. (2003). *Is the Rainbow Seven Colors or Six? Thinking about the Problem of Truth and Education*. Kasetsusha.

Iyengar, S. (2010). *The Art of Choosing*. Hachette, UK.

Japan Color Research Institute. (1954). *Color Name Dictionary*. Tokyo Sogensha.

JIS Z 8102:2001 Names of Non-Luminous Object Colours.

JIS Z 8105:2000 Glossary of Colour Terms

REFERENCES   181

Jo, K. (Ed.). (2015). *Color de toured Japan and the World: Colors of Life, Spring, Summer, Autumn, Winter*. Seigensha.

Johnson, P. (1987). *A History of the Jews*. Harper & Row.

Kamekura, Y., Ogawa, M., Tanaka, I., & Nagai, K. (Eds). (2005). *Yusaku Kamekura's Design*. Rokuyosha.

Kandinsky, W. (2012, originally 1912). *Concerning the spiritual in art*. Courier Corporation.

Kariya, T., & Hanasaki, A. (1987). *Oishinbo a la Carte 13*. Shogakukan.

Kay, P., & McDaniel, C. K. (1975). Color Categories as Fuzzy Sets. Language Behavior Research Laboratory, University of California. https://eric.ed.gov/?id=ED138093

Kay, P., Berlin, B., Maffi, L., Merrifield, W. R., & Cook, R. (2009). *The World Color Survey*. CSLI Publications.

Kepler, J. (1596–1609). *The Harmony of the Universe: An Enduring Cosmology*. Originally written in Latin. (2009, Kishimoto Trans.). Kosakusha.

Kikai Kanran. (1827). (Reprint 1978).

Kitagami, S., et al. (2010). Does Color Matter for Toilet Marks? (2): A Comparative Cultural Examination of Stroop-like Effects in the Recognition of Toilet Marks. *Proceedings of the Japanese Association of Cognitive Psychology*.

Kuehni, R. G., & Schwarz, A. (2008). *Color Ordered: A Survey of Color Systems from Antiquity to the Present*. Oxford University Press.

Kunimoto, N. (2009). The Color Red in 8th Century Japan. *Journal of the Color Science Association of Japan, 33*(3), (pp. 251–262).

Kuriki, I., Lange, R., Muto, Y., Brown, A. M., Fukuda, K., Tokunaga, R., Lindsey, D. T., Uchikawa, K., & Shioiri, S. (2017). The Modern Japanese Color Lexicon. *Journal of Vision, 17*(3), (p. 1).

Lenneberg, E. H., & Roberts, J. M. (1956). *The Language of Experience: A Study in Methodology*. Massachusetts Institute of Technology, Center for International Studies.

Lévi-Strauss, C. (1976). *La Pensée Sauvage* (Japanese translation). (Originally in French, Ohashi, Trans.). Misuzu shobo.

Lévi-Strauss, C., & Eribon, D. (2008). *Conversations with Claude Levi-Strauss* (Originally in French, Takeuchi, Trans.). Misuzu shobo.

MacDonald, L. W., Biggam, C. P., & Paramei, G. V. (2018). *Progress in Colour Studies: Cognition, Language and Beyond*. John Benjamins Publishing Company.

MacLaury, R. E. (1997). Skewing and Darkening: Dynamics of the Cool Category. In C. Hardin & L. Maffi (Eds.), *Color Categories in Thought and Language* (pp. 261–282). Cambridge: Cambridge University Press.

MacLaury, R. E. (1997). *Color and Cognition in Mesoamerica: Constructing Categories as Vantages* (Vol. 10). University of Texas Press.

182 REFERENCES

MacLaury, R. E., Paramei, G. V., & Dedrick, D. (2007). *Anthropology of Color: Interdisciplinary Multilevel Modeling*. John Benjamins Publishing Company.

Madden, T. J., Hewett, K., & Roth, M. S. (2000). Managing Images in Different Cultures: A Cross-National Study of Color Meanings and Preferences. *Journal of International Marketing, 8*(4), (pp. 90–107).

Maeda, U. (1980). *Color: Dye and Color* (Mono to Ningen no Bunka Shi 38). Hosei University Press.

Maeda, Y. (1956). *Murasaki-kusa–Japanese Colors: A Cultural and Historical Study*. Kawade Shobo.

Maeda, Y. (1960). *A History of Japanese Color Culture*. Iwanami Shoten.

Maerz, A., & Rea Paul, M. (1950). *A Dictionary of Color* (2nd ed.). New York, Toronto, London: McGraw-Hill Book Company.

Mandela, N. (2014). *The Long Road to Freedom: The Autobiography of Nelson Mandela* (Japanese translation by Agarie, K.). NHK Publishing (e-book).

Matanski, V. (2015). Generative Visualization Based on Sound. Conference: Doctoral Conference in Mathematics and Informatics, Sofia, Bulgaria.

Matsuyama, S., et al. (2020). A Survey of Color and Sound Associations Using the App "mupic". *Journal of the Color Science Association of Japan, 44*(3+), p. 74.

McComb, L. (2012, October). Pharrell William's Extraordinary Gift. *The Oprah Magazine*.

McDermott, K. (2002). "To blanch an Ethiop": Jonson's Masque of Blackness and Multicultural English Literature. *Language Arts Journal of Michigan, 18*(1), Article 5, p. 20.

Minaka, N. (2017). *Systematics of Thinking: Diagrammology from the View of Classification and Systematics*. Shunju-sha.

Mitsuboshi, M. (Ed.). *Color Symbols of the World: Aspects of Nature, Language, and Culture*. Ochanomizu Shobo.

Miyahara, E. (2003). Focal Colors and Unique Hues. *Perceptual and Motor Skills, 97*(3 Pt 2).

Mogi, K. (2006). *Qualia of Food*. Seidosha.

Moon, P., & Spencer, D. E. (1944). Aesthetic Measure Applied to Color Harmony. *JOSA, 34*(4).

Mori, M. (2022). *An Introduction to Heraldry*. Chikuma Shobo.

Munsell, A. H. (1967). *A Color Notation* (12th ed.). Munsell Color Company.

Munsell Color Company. (1929). *Munsell Book of Color*. Baltimore.

Nagasaki, S. (1996). *Traditional Colors of Japan: Their Color Names and Color Tones* (Kyoto Shoin Arts Collection 5). Kyoto shoin.

Naito, T., & Gielen, U. P. (1992). *Tatemae* and *honne*: A Study of Moral Relativism in Japanese Culture. *Psychology in International Perspective, 50*, (pp. 161–172).

REFERENCES   183

Newman, W. R. (2018). *Newton the Alchemist: Science, Enigma, and the Quest for Nature's "Secret Fire"*. Princeton University Press.

Newton. I. (1983). *Opticks* (N. Shimao, Trans.). Iwanami Shoten.

Nicolle, D. (1984). *Arthur and the Anglo-Saxon War*. Osprey Publishing, p. 21.

Nikkei Design (Ed.). (2012). *Textbook for ackage Design*. Nikkei BP.

Nishida, T. (2007). *Where Did Humanity Come From: An Approach from Primate Studies*. Kyoto University Press.

Nutrition Improvement Promotion Association (Ed.). (1990). *We Love Rice*.

Obayashi, T. (1999). *Ginga no Michi: Niji no Kakehashi (The Way of the Galaxy: Bridging the Rainbow)*. Shogakukan.

Ogata, K. (2001). Color Names of the Rainbow. *Color Forum Japan 2001*, edited by The Four Societies of Optics.

Okimori, K. (2010). A Historical Study of Color Language. Oufu.

Okuda, H., et al. (2002). Correlation between the Image of Food Colors and the Taste Sense: The Case of Japanese Twenties. *Journal of Cookery Science of Japan, 35* (1), (pp. 2–9).

Omi, G. (1983). *A History of Color and World Affairs*. Shiseido.

Ono, A., et al. (2010). Investigation and Analysis of Color Vocabulary for the Modern Japanese. *Journal of the Color Science Society of Japan, 34*(1), (pp. 2–13).

Parole der Woche. (1942, July 1).

Pastoureau, M. (2008). *Black: The History of a Color*. Princeton University Press.

Pastoureau, M. (1995). *The Colors of Europe* (Ishii & Nozaki, Trans.). Papyrus.

Peel, J. (2006). The Scale and the Spectrum. *Cabinet*. Winter (22). Retrieved 28 November 2016.

Rabelais, F. (1991). *Rabelais's First Book: Pantagruel, The Very Horrific Life of Great Gargantua, Father of Pantagruel*. (Watanabe, Trans.). Iwanami Shoten.

Robbins, K. (Ed.). (2013). *Oxford History of the British Isles*. Keio University Press.

Rothstein, R. (2017). *The Color of Law: A Forgotten History of How Our Government Segregated America* (1st ed.). Liveright.

Sahlins, M. (Ed.). (1960). Evolution and Culture. "Chapter 3: Adaptation and Stability" (pp. 45–68). University of Michigan Press.

Sahlins, M. (1976). Colors and Cultures, *Semiotica* 16:1, Mouton Publishers (pp. 1–22).

Saini, A. (2019). *Superior: The Return of Race Science*. Fourth Estate.

Sanders, R., & Salerno, S. (2018). *Pride: The Story of Harvey Milk and the Rainbow Flag*. Random House Books for Young Readers.

Saunders, B. (1995). Disinterring Basic Color Terms: A Study in the Mystique of Cognitivism. *History of the Human Sciences, 8*(4), (pp. 19–38).

Saunders, B. (2000). Revisiting Basic Color Terms. *The Journal of the Royal Anthropological Institute, 6*(1), (pp. 81–99).

184   REFERENCES

Saunders, B. (2006). The Normativity of Colour. In Carole P. Biggam & Christian J. Kay (Eds.), *Progress in Colour Studies: Volume I. Language and Culture* (pp. 88–99). John Benjamins Publishing Company.

Saunders, B. A. C., & Van Brakel, J. (2001). Rewriting Color. *Philosophy of the Social Sciences, 31*(4), (pp. 538–566).

Schier, D. S. (1941). *Louis Bertrand Castel, Anti-Newtonian Scientist*. The Torch Press.

Schlintl, C., & Schienle, A. (2020). Effects of Coloring Food Images on the Propensity to Eat: A Placebo Approach with Color Suggestions. *Frontiers in Psychology, 11*, (p. 589826).

Schumm, L. (2010). Six Times M&Ms Made History. https://www.history.com/news/the-wartime-origins-of-the-mm

Shakespeare, W. (1980). *Shakespeare's Complete Works 7* (Odajima trans.). Hakusuisha.

Shakespeare, W. (1989). *Titus Andronicus* (Kinoshita trans.). Kodansha.

Shimada, H. (2016). The Age of One Man's Religion. *History of Religious Events as a Culticulture*. Kawade bunko.

Stanlaw, J. (1997). Two Observations on Culture Contact and the Japanese Color Nomenclature System. In C. L. Hardin & Luisa Maffi (Eds.), *Color Categories in Thought and Language* (pp. 240–260). Cambridge University Press.

Stevenson, R. L. (1901). *Vailima Letters*. Scribner's Bookstore.

Sugagawa, S. (1999). *Meaning and Metaphor of English Color Words: A Historical Study*. Seibidō.

Sugita Y. (2004). Experience in Early Infancy is Indispensable for Color Perception. *Current Biology: CB 14*(14), (pp. 1267–1271).

Sugiyama, K. (2013). *A Picture History of the Rainbow*. Kawade Shobo Shinsha.

Suzuki, T. (1990). *Japanese and Foreign Languages*. Iwanami Shoten.

Tagawa, S. (1969). *Norakuro Platoon Commander*. Kodansha (original in 1936).

Takemoto, K., et al. (1986). *The Etymology of Chemistry*. Kagaku Dojin.

Taniguchi, M. (1989). Kunio Yanagida's Hare Ke Theory. *Kunio Yanagita and Shinobu Orikuchi: Between Learning and Creation*, edited by Hiromitsu Takahashi. Yuseido.

Terashima, R. (1985). *Wakan Sansai Zue* (Trans. and annotated by I. Shimada et al.). Heibonsha.

The Associated Press. (2007, June 19). Papers Show Isaac Newton's Religious Side, Predict Date of Apocalypse.

The Color Science Association of Japan (Ed.). (2006). Color in Life. Color Science Course 2 (pp. 156–162).

The Oxford English Dictionary, Second Edition (1989). Clarendon Press. Definition 9, p. 239.

Tseng, C., et al. (1997). Semantics in Chinese color language: A Study of Red from *"Houn Rou Mon"* of Ching Dynasty. *Proceedings of the Annual Conference of JSSD, 44* (p. 74). https://doi.org/10.11247/jssd.44.0_74

Tsutada, N. (2010). "People Living in Ancient Times: A Visit to the Bodhi People of Ethiopia." AFRO SPACE homepage: https://www.afrospace.info/Ethiopia-Bodi.htm

Turner, V. (1967). *The Forest of Symbols: Aspects of the Ndembu Ritual.* Cornell University Press.

Utsumi, M., Kobayashi, S., & Sakai, F. (2006). A Study on the Institutional Transition from Landscape Ordinance to Landscape Law: A Case Study of Odawara City, Kanagawa Prefecture. *City Planning Review, 41,* (pp. 319–324).

Van Gogh, V. (Year unknown). *Letter 497.* Amsterdam: Van Gogh Museum.

Van Norden, L. (1985). *The Black Feet of the Peacock: The Color-Concept 'Black' from the Greeks Through the Renaissance.* University Press of America.

Van Wijk, H. A. C. W. (1959). A Cross-Cultural Theory of Colour and Brightness Nomenclature. *Bijdragen tot de Taal-, Land- en Volkenkunde / Journal of the Humanities and Social Sciences of Southeast Asia and Oceania, 115,* (April 1959, Bijdragen tot de Ta2).

Whitman, J. Q. (2017). *Hitler's American Model: The United States and the Making of Nazi Race Law.* Princeton University Press.

Wierzbicka, A. (2006). *The Semantics of Colour: A New Paradigm.* In C. P. Biggam & C. J. Kay (Eds.), *Progress in Colour Studies: Volume I. Language and culture.* John Benjamins Publishing Company.

Wildman, S. M. (1996). *Privilege Revealed: How Invisible Preference Undermines America.* NYU Press.

Winawer, J., Witthoft, N., Frank, M. C., Wu, L., Wade, A. R., & Boroditsky, L. (2007). Russian Blues Reveal the Effects of Language on Color Discrimination. *PNAS, 104*(19), (pp. 7780–7785).

Yamamoto, M. (Ed.). (1969). *The Complete Works of Aristotle 10.* Iwanami Shoten.

University of Tokyo Sogo Kenkyukai (Ed.). (2001). *Dividing* (Wakeru, University of Tokyo Open Lecture 73). University of Tokyo Press.

Yomiuri Shinbun. (2015, July 31).

Yoshioka, Y. (2000). *A Dictionary of Japanese Colors.* Shikosha.

Yu, H. (Producer). (2016). *China's van Goghs.*

INDEX

A
Achromatic, 5, 36, 103, 106, 107, 118, 120, 123
Additive color mixing, 24, 75
Afterimage, 76, 84
Andrews, David, 50, 52, 95
Anthropology, 4, 12, 16, 37–41, 49, 65, 66, 69, 96, 150
Apartheid, 148, 149, 152, 175
Apelles of Kos, 74
Aristotle, 74, 161
Aryan, 152, 154
Attention, 49, 95, 148
Attributes, 5, 11, 20, 38, 72, 74, 77, 81, 83–85, 89, 96, 98, 99, 137, 175
Ayers, Nathaniel, 111
Azuma Kagami, 16, 19

B
Baker, Gilbert, 32
Basic Color Categories (BCC), 4, 42
Basic color terms (BCT), 4, 37, 40, 41, 43–46, 50, 52–57, 60, 63, 65, 66, 68, 69, 94, 98, 108, 159, 175
Bassa, 21, 22
Benczes, R., 53
Berlin, B., 4, 39–41, 43–47, 54–58, 60, 65–69, 71, 72, 77, 79, 94, 98–100, 108, 175
Biggam, Carole P., 42, 50, 56, 159, 173
Bilingual, 39, 51–53, 55, 95
Birren, Faber, 127
Black, 5, 18, 24, 30, 41, 43, 44, 50, 57, 58, 60, 61, 72–80, 83, 89, 97, 98, 101, 103, 106–108, 110, 120, 123, 124, 135, 137–139, 141, 143, 147–151, 154, 157, 159–162, 165, 167
Black Lives Matter (#Black Lives Matter, BLM), 166
Blue, 1, 2, 5, 6, 8, 16, 19, 20, 22, 23, 28, 33, 37, 41–43, 47, 50–57, 60–62, 69, 72–80, 93–95, 97, 101, 103, 105–107, 117–120, 124–129, 134, 135,

© The Editor(s) (if applicable) and The Author(s), under exclusive
license to Springer Nature Switzerland AG 2024
K. Hidaka, *The Art of Color Categorization*,
https://doi.org/10.1007/978-3-031-47690-7

188 INDEX

137–139, 141, 143, 152, 154, 161, 174, 175
Blumenbach, Johann Friedrich, 150, 151
Bodi, 100–102, 134
Body colors, 133, 148
Boundaries, 40–45, 52, 95, 99, 106
Boys' color, 106
Brewster, David, 75, 77, 80
British Colour Council (BCC), 59
Brown, 8, 41, 43, 60, 61, 97, 101, 105, 116, 118, 123–125, 130, 137, 139–142, 145, 150–152
Brown, Pierce, 133, 134

C

Castel, Louis-Bertrand, 26
Caucasoid, 150
Celtic, 56
Chagall, Marc, 71
Cheskin, Lewis, 117
Chevreul, Michel-Eugène, 30
Chomsky, Avram Noam, 67, 68
Classification, 4, 20–23, 36, 50, 51, 67, 94–98, 100, 102, 106, 108, 139, 145, 150, 175
Coat of arms, 134, 135
Cole, Teju, 168
Color blindness, 69, 70
Color card, 100–102
Color category, 40, 45, 50, 94, 95
Color chart, 11, 12, 38–44, 46, 47, 53, 63, 64, 67, 68, 72, 77, 79, 81, 88, 89, 91, 99, 100, 121, 125, 144, 152, 154, 156, 175
Color culture, 12, 49, 102, 117, 173, 174
Colored, 2, 6, 23, 24, 26, 77, 86, 101, 102, 105, 107, 111, 116, 124, 127, 148, 164
Colorful, 1
Color harmony, 144

Color hearing, 109
Color mixing, 76, 77, 83
Color names, 4, 5, 11, 12, 16, 36, 37, 39, 43, 49, 50, 52–54, 57–65, 68, 69, 71, 72, 81–83, 95, 97, 98, 100, 101, 137, 140–143, 166, 175
Color rendering, 46
Color revolution, 63
Color scheme, 7, 11, 64, 84, 100, 105, 106, 118–121, 124, 126, 128, 134, 137, 140, 141, 144, 174
Color solid, 44, 84
Color space, 42, 81, 85, 86, 99
Color sphere, 44, 77, 85, 89
Color system, 11, 77, 81–86, 89, 163, 166
Color temperature, 46, 47, 49, 79, 80, 94
Color theory, 12, 19, 23, 25, 26, 71, 75, 94
Color vision, 7, 8, 11, 36, 65, 69, 175
Color wheel, 71, 77, 83, 84, 129, 152
Communication, 4, 23, 37, 61, 62, 69, 81, 143, 176
Communitas, 108
Complementary colors, 76, 84
Conklin, Harold Collier, 96, 97, 100
Contrasting color/opposite color, 59, 71, 76, 77, 83, 135
Conventional color name, 36, 37, 68
Cool, 6, 93–96, 125
Count Gobineau, Joseph Arthur de, 150
Cultural relativism, 38, 98
Cultural universals, 41, 174, 175
Cyan, magenta, yellow, and black (CMYK), 75, 77, 78

INDEX 189

D
Darwin, Charles, 67, 149
Dass, Angélica, 147
Da Vinci, Leonardo, 76
Decorum, 144
Descartes, René, 24
Diversity, 6, 7, 11, 12, 33, 38, 43, 48, 66, 68, 102, 147, 152, 173, 174
Dorr, Robert, 93
Durkheim, Emile, 104

E
Edison, Thomas, 168
Einstein, Albert, 2
English, 4, 12, 20, 21, 23, 25, 38, 39, 49–52, 54–56, 58–61, 64, 66, 75, 78, 83, 93, 96, 102, 124, 125, 148, 159, 161–163
Environmental light, 46, 47
Estonian, 52, 53
Ethnocentric, 98
Eugenics, 149, 151, 152, 175
Everett, Daniel, 57, 58
Everyday life, 2, 104–106, 108, 109
Evolution, 6, 38, 40, 41, 56, 67, 68, 95, 96, 149, 152
Eye color, 58, 66, 152

F
Family crest, 135
Festivals, 103, 104, 106, 174
Fischer, Eugen, 150
Five colors (Goshiki), 16, 18–20, 25, 72, 73
Floyd, George, 166, 167
Focal color, 4, 39–42, 44, 45, 55, 56, 60, 79, 94, 95
Food, 3, 8, 37, 49, 70, 81, 91, 101, 102, 104–106, 115–117, 125–131, 174

Forty-eight browns and a Hundred Rats, 142, 143
Four-color palette, 75
Four seasons, 97, 102, 140, 141
Frank, Anne, 175
Fraunhofer lines, 30, 33, 42
Fukui, Katsuyoshi, 6, 100–103
Fukuzawa, Yukichi, 151

G
Gender, 33, 69, 70, 94, 106, 107, 109, 174
German, 20, 26, 30, 48, 75, 76, 78, 127, 137, 150, 151, 154, 155, 157
Girls' color, 106
Gladstone, William Ewart, 66, 67
Gleason, Henry Alan, 21, 22
Goethe, Johann Wolfgang von, 28, 79, 80, 94, 173
Good and evil, 161
Göring, Hermann Wilhelm, 157
Gray, 5, 8, 41, 43, 44, 56, 57, 60, 61, 76, 77, 83, 85, 89, 97, 101, 103, 118, 120, 123–125, 135, 141, 142, 145, 152
Greater Pliny, 74
Green, 1, 2, 5–7, 16, 18–20, 23, 28, 33, 37, 41–43, 47, 54–57, 60, 62, 69, 71–73, 75–81, 86, 94, 95, 97, 101, 103, 105, 110, 116–120, 123–126, 129, 131, 134, 135, 137, 142, 143, 148, 152, 175
GRUE, 56
Günther, Hans, 150

H
Hale Color Consultants, 44, 46
Hanunóo, 44, 96–98, 100, 104
Hare and *ke*, 103–106, 108, 140

190 INDEX

Harmony, 62, 144
Helmholtz, Hermann von, 75
Hering, Ewald, 76
Hermann grid illusion, 44
Hidaka, Toshitaka, 23
Hierarchy, 78, 139, 152, 163, 168
Himmler, Heinrich Luitpold, 154
Hippocrates of Kos, 74
Hisano, Ai, 127
Hitler, Adolf, 154
Hoffman, Johann Leonhard, 28, 29
Homer, 66, 67
Hue, 38, 42, 44, 46, 50, 53, 56, 62,
    78–81, 83–86, 88, 89, 96–98,
    117, 118, 123–126, 142–144
Humidity, 94, 96
Hungarian, 53, 54, 81

I

I can't breathe, 166
Indigo dye, 50
Industrialization, 83, 127
Institutional (organizational) racism,
    152
Iyengar, Sheena, 35

J

Jackson, Michael, 159
Japanese, 2, 4, 5, 8, 12, 18, 19,
    22–26, 29, 38, 39, 42, 43, 45,
    48–50, 53–64, 66, 69, 80, 94,
    96, 97, 101–104, 106, 107, 115,
    119, 120, 123–130, 135,
    137–144, 147, 151, 157, 166
Jewish, 116, 150, 154, 157, 174, 175
Jim Crow laws, 152, 159, 163, 164

K

Kandinsky, Vasily, 28, 29, 109

Kay, P., 4, 39–41, 43–47, 54–58, 60,
    65–69, 71, 72, 77, 79, 94,
    98–100, 108, 175
Kepler, Johannes, 24, 26
Kikai Kanran, 29
Kircher, Athanasius, 26
Kitabatake, Akira, 44
Kuriki, Ichiro, 45, 46, 99

L

Landscape laws, 144, 145
Lauper, Cyndi, 93
Lebensborn, 154
Lenneberg, Eric Heinz, 38, 39, 44,
    95, 99
Lévi-Strauss, Claude, 49, 96, 97, 150
LGBTQ+, 32, 33
Lighting (illumination), 5, 15, 46–48,
    79, 121, 127, 128, 140, 173
Liminality, 108
Linguistic relativism, 21, 38, 39, 41,
    54, 58, 60, 65–67, 96, 98, 99
Liszt, Franz, 109
Loan words, 57, 59–61
Loitšenko, Olga, 52, 53, 95

M

Meiji, 22, 23, 61, 64, 145, 151, 152
Mixed blood, 154, 164
Mixed colors, 43, 76, 78, 79, 98
Miyazawa, Kenji, 109
Mongoloid, 150
Morale, 102, 134
Munsell color chart, 38, 43–46, 48,
    79, 81, 89, 99
Munsell Color Company, 38, 44, 81,
    82, 89, 91, 99, 145
Munsell color system, 77, 81, 84–86
Music scales, 26

N

Nabokov, Vladimir, 109
Natural Color System (NCS), 79
Nazis, 152, 154, 155, 157, 163
Ndembu, 107, 108
Neapolitan cake, 116
Nemcsics, Antal, 81
Newton's disk, 77
Newton, Isaac, 20, 23–26, 28, 29, 76, 77
Nishida, Toshisada, 70, 174
Non-Aryan race/race, 154
Norden, Van, 160
Number of colors of the rainbow, 30
Nuremberg, 168
Nuremberg Laws, 154, 157
Nuremberg trials, 168

O

Obayashi, Taryo, 16, 19, 20
Ocular harpsichord, 26, 27
Ogata, Koji, 22, 23
Oishinbo a la Carte, 115
Okimori, Kumi, 59, 60
Opposite (contrasting, complementary) colors, 71, 76, 77, 83, 135
Orphism, 29
Osaka, Naomi, 166, 167
Ostwald color system, 83, 84
Ostwald, Friedrich, 78, 79, 98

P

Package, 11, 91, 119–121, 123–128, 149
Pastoureau, Michel, 160, 161
Perkin, William, 88
Perspective theory, 144
Pink, 2, 5, 33, 41, 43, 50, 56, 60, 61, 103, 106, 107, 116, 118, 125, 142, 143

Pirahã, 57, 58
Post, Richard, 65
Preferred color, 129
Pride flag, 33
Primary color, 42, 72–78, 80, 89, 138
Prohibited colors, 135, 139
Psychology, 4, 12, 36, 41, 76, 109, 159
Pure blood, 154
Pure colors, 43, 78, 79, 83, 89, 149
Purple, 5, 16, 22, 28, 33, 37, 41–43, 49, 56, 60, 61, 71, 75, 77, 80, 88, 94, 97, 101, 103, 118, 123, 125, 134, 135, 137–139, 141, 142, 148

R

Race, 58, 65, 68, 69, 134, 147, 148, 150–152, 154, 157, 159, 162–165, 175
Racial science, 150
Racial segregation policies, 68, 152
Racism, 11, 148–150, 152, 163–166, 175
Rainbow, 11, 15–27, 29–31, 33, 42, 64, 72, 76, 81, 84, 89, 116
Rainbow cookies, 116
Rainbow flag, 32, 33
Rank, 11, 72, 79, 80, 89, 107, 138, 139, 141, 149, 175
Rat/gray, 60, 61, 142
Rat color, 142
Red, 1, 3, 5–7, 16, 18–20, 22, 23, 25, 28, 29, 33, 37, 39, 41–43, 47, 48, 50, 53, 54, 56, 57, 60, 62, 63, 69, 71–82, 84, 86, 94, 97, 101–103, 105–109, 117, 119, 120, 123–127, 129–131, 134, 135, 137–139, 141, 142, 145, 148, 150, 151, 159, 165, 174, 175
Redlining, 163–165

192 INDEX

Red Rising, 133, 134
Remaining colors, 124
Retinal cells, 76
Rimbaud, Arthur, 110, 111
Rood, Ogden Nicholas, 83
Rotational color mixing, 76, 77, 83
Runge, Philippe Otto, 85
Russian, 20, 28, 50–53

S
Sahlins, Marshall, 6, 7
Salient, 39, 41, 79
Sandford, Jodi L., 159, 160
Sapir, Edward, 38, 39, 41, 58, 60
Saturation, 38, 44, 81, 85, 86, 88,
    89, 96, 98, 119, 123, 128, 138,
    144, 145
Saunders, B.A.C., 99, 148
Scriabin, Alexander, 109
Secondary colors, 75, 80
Seven colors, 18–20, 22, 23, 25, 26,
    29, 41, 64, 105, 116, 141
Shakespeare, William, 162
Shona, 21
Six colors, 20, 21, 23, 33, 43, 76,
    139, 141
Skin, 11, 41, 44, 58, 60, 93, 103,
    139, 147–149, 151, 152, 154,
    159, 163–166, 168, 174–176
Social evolution, 38
Spanish, 55, 61, 95
Spencer, Herbert Hippocrates, 149
Staining, 135
Standard light source, 46, 47
Stereotypes, 2, 5, 68, 69, 106, 107,
    117, 151, 168
Stevenson, Robert Lewis, 82
Stroop effect, 107
Sugiyama, Kunihiko, 20, 23
Sumptuary laws, 64, 141, 142, 145
Superiority, 150, 152, 154, 163, 175

Suzuki, Takao, 19–21
Synchromism, 29
Synesthetes, 29, 109

T
Tagalog, 61
Takanawa Ushimachi, 19, 20
Temperament, 25, 74
Temperature, 22, 79, 94, 95
Terashima, Ryoan, 17
Tertiary colors, 75, 80
Tetrachromatikón, 75
The Diary of Anne Frank, 175
The Hungry Caterpillar, 54
The Japanese Industrial Standards, 36
Theory of Color, 28, 79, 80, 94
Theory of linguistic universals, 68
The Yellow Emperor's Inner, 73
Three attributes, 77, 81, 83, 85, 96,
    98, 99
Three colors, 20, 21, 33, 108, 116
Three primary colors, 75, 77
Threshold, 42, 108
Tóth-Czifra, E., 53
Traditional color, 37, 50, 59, 61, 63,
    64, 174
Tree of colors, 88, 89
True colors, 93
Turner, Victor, 107, 108
Two-dimensional color system, 84
Two seasons, 97
Tzeltal, 40, 47, 55

U
Unique hue, 78, 79
Utagawa (Ando) Hiroshige, 18

V
Van Gogh, Vincent Willem, 7, 8, 47
Visibility, 134

INDEX 193

W

Warm, 6, 22, 71, 93–96, 98, 106, 123, 127, 128
Weddings and funerals, 104, 141
Werner's *Nomenclature of Colours*, 67
White, 3, 5, 18, 19, 24, 41, 43, 44, 49, 50, 57, 58, 60, 61, 72–76, 78–80, 83, 89, 96, 98, 101, 103, 105–108, 117, 118, 120, 124, 125, 130, 135, 138, 139, 147–151, 154, 159–161, 164–168
White Australia, 152
White rainbow, 17
White Savior Industrial Complex, 168
White supremacy, 151, 163
Whitman, James, 154, 157
Whorf, Benjamin Lee, 38, 39, 41, 58, 60
Wierzbicka, Anna, 4, 108
Williams, Farrell, 109

Winawer, Jonathan, 52, 95
Wonder, Stevie, 109
World Color Survey, 43

Y

Yanagita, Kunio, 103, 105
Yellow, 1, 3, 5, 8, 16, 19, 22, 23, 28, 29, 33, 37, 39, 41, 43, 47, 57, 60, 71–80, 84, 93, 94, 97, 101, 103, 105, 110, 117–119, 123–125, 128–131, 135, 137–139, 141, 150, 151, 157, 174
Yellow base/blue base, 93
Yoshioka, Yukio, 140
Young, Thomas, 75

Z

Zuni, 38, 39

Printed in the United States
by Baker & Taylor Publisher Services